THE EMERGENT CHURCH

Undefining Christianity

Bob DeWaay

The Emergent Church – Undefining Christianity

Copyright © 2009 Bob DeWaay

Published by
Bob DeWaay
2610 Xenwood Avenue South
Saint Louis Park, MN 55416

Cover design by Bryan Anderson
Theological Abstracts by K. Jentoft
Interior design by Bethany Press International
Printed by Bethany Press International.

ISBN: 978-0-578-00999-5

All Scripture taken from the New American Standard Bible, © Copyright 1960, 1962, 1963, 1968, 1971, 1972, 1973, 1975, 1977, 1988, 1995 The Lockman Foundation.
Used by Permission

Printed in the United States of America. All rights reserved under International Copyright Law. May not be reproduced in any form without permission in writing from the Publisher.

Table of Contents

Preface

During his lifetime, Francis A. Schaeffer fought courageously and compassionately to defend orthodox Christianity from the ideas that that now are labeled "postmodern" or "emergent." He taught and wrote that the only way to preserve a Christianity of reason that truthfully addressed all of life was to adopt *sola scriptura*, the Reformation view of the Scriptures. Because of my high regard for Schaeffer and his position, and my firm belief that his teaching holds true today, I am dedicating this book to his memory.

Each decade of my Christian life—the 1970s, 80s, and 90s—as well as the present time, I have read and re-read his trilogy *The God Who is There*, *Escape from Reason*, and *He is There and He is not Silent*. These works continue to apply to the important issues facing the church today; in fact, his writing is more important today than ever before. Schaeffer warned about the despair that results when ideas take us away from the validity of God's self-revelation in Scripture. The Emergent attempts to hide this despair by a philosophical leap of faith that springs from Hegel. I continue to read Schaeffer; his argument still prevails, and, as a result, you will find citations from Schaeffer's writings in many of the chapters of this book.

In his day, Schaeffer and many others like him stood for *sola scriptura* and fought the battle for the Bible when theological trends threatened to undermine it. Schaeffer and his fellows issued the "Chicago Statement on Biblical Inerrancy" in 1978. Today, as postmodern theology undermines Biblical authority, many who signed the Chicago Statement have passed from the scene of history, and few have taken their place to sound the alarm.

Now into this silent void comes postmodern teaching. Young people are told that they must accept postmodernity's premises because the Reformation view with regard to knowing truth has met its demise. The teaching of Emergent offers spiritual experiences as a replacement for truth. Having no real scriptural base, these young people are being seduced and deluded. But there is hope. The truth *can* be known because God has spoken and can be understood. His words are meaningful both to Him and to Bible readers. We simply must break through that intellectual clutter with the truth of the scriptures.

This book represents my best effort to point us to the gospel itself and to confess that God has spoken once for all in Scripture. You will find that frequently I call upon Schaeffer's writings, and it will be apparent why when you see what he has to say about these matters.

May the Lord raise up young people who are not mesmerized by Emergent and postmodern subjectivity who will instead fight the good fight of the faith for the next generation.

Bob DeWaay
January 2009

WHY THEY ARE NECESSARY

Each chapter of this book will be accompanied by a theological abstract that will explain the content and argument of the chapter. The abstracts are necessary. Many of the concepts covered in this book are complicated, especially for those who have limited experience with the 21st century postmodern philosophical thinking and phraseology. In order to deal adequately with the beliefs of the Emergent Church the author has had to interact with these complex ideas, their historical context, and their implications. These abstracts explain in a simple, straightforward, summary manner what the Emergent Church promotes and what its theology and teachings imply.

UNDERSTANDING THE CONTRADICTORY

Emergent theology has been very difficult to categorize and understand precisely because its leaders hold diverse and even opposing positions on nearly every major Christian doctrine. Confusing though their theology may be, we still can understand and evaluate whether or not the Emergent Church's core beliefs are true or false. Emergent leaders work hard to obscure the foundations of their beliefs, and they constantly seek to promote their ideas as "new and unique." This book will demonstrate that these ideas are neither new nor unique. When a believer of absolutes studies the positions promoted by Emergent church leaders the believer may find those positions impossible to understand, irrational, or even silly. In this book we will explain the Emergent paradigm and why, once one accepts the Emergent foundations, the system actually can seem rational and understandable. And once it is understandable we can discern whether or not it is true.

Introduction

THE EMERGENT CHURCH - Undefining Christianity

In January 2006 our congregation, Twin City Fellowship, hosted a debate between a top Emergent leader, Doug Pagitt, and I entitled The Emergent Church and Postmodern Spirituality. For the first time in the 27 years our congregation had been meeting at that particular location in south Minneapolis we packed the place; nearly 500 people attended. Most people came to find out what the Emergent Church is all about. Many from Pagitt's own congregation came to find out why and on what basis I thought they were in error. It was the first time that a leader of the Emergent "conversation" had debated a traditionalist, and it turned out to be quite an evening.

The format we agreed upon allowed for each of us each to give a 20-minute opening presentation. Pagitt used his time to present 11 characteristics of the Emergent Church.[1] These points were noteworthy because of their ability to intrigue and yet not really inform.

---

1 Pagitt's Eleven Points

Kingdom of-God focused, and we want to join the kingdom of God wherever we find it.
We are pursuing faithfulness through new practices, structures and understandings.
We have a hopeful and positive view of God's engagement in the world (there is a rhythm of God in the world and we should find it and join in it).
We are committed to loving God, neighbor and enemy in real ways.
We are deeply connected to the story of God and the Bible.
We are living with the guidance of the Holy Spirit (experiencing the ongoing creation of God).
We are theologically active.
We are open to "the other."
We want the good news of Jesus to change the world and be good news for all of creation.
We understand community to be an essential part of a Christian life.
We are interested in the future more than fighting the battles of the past - more future oriented than "left or right," liberal or conservative.

These are drawn from his Microsoft PowerPoint presentation and explanations given at the debate.

For example, that the Emergent Church is kingdom of God-focused is a meaningless term unless one knows what their definition of the kingdom actually is. Pagitt's explanation suggests that the kingdom of God is somewhere to be found by those who know what they are looking for. But how does one look for that which is undefined? That issue went unresolved.

Many who attended the debate noticed this and expressed frustration. One person commented, "I came here to find out what the Emerging Church is all about, I listened for three hours, and I still do not know what the Emerging Church believes." Over the course of my study I have found that vagaries are the nuts and bolts of the Emergent "conversation." The rhythm of God in the world sounds like an attractive thing to find, but what is it? The frustration that many experienced at the debate and in their own study of the movement is due to the fact that Emergent leaders loathe definitions. Definitions create boundaries, they say, and boundaries keep people out.

I find that Emergent Church leaders do their best *not* to be understood, suggesting that being clever, coy, contradictory, or even provocative is a better way to help people emerge from old categories of thought into new, synthetic ones. The debate revealed that tendency. Pagitt is a very nice man who is funny, self deprecating, friendly, and winsome. But debating him was an exercise in futility. It was as though we were playing checkers and chess at the same time and on the same board. Theologically and philosophically we really were in two different worlds.

My worldview is comprised of defined categories that help us understand truth and express it in meaningful words. Words convey meaning validly, even across cultural and language barriers. We can know the words that the Biblical writers penned, and in knowing them we are accountable to them as God's authoritative expression of His will, His revelation of His nature, and that of the world He created. God's words draw boundaries between truth and error, good and evil, sin and righteousness. God's words hold us accountable for future judgment. In my opening statement, I cited this verse: "*He who rejects Me and does not receive My sayings, has one who judges him; the word I spoke is what will judge him at the last day*" (**John 12:48**).

I further explained that Jesus' authoritative words draw boundaries and that our status in the future judgment will be determined by where we stand in relationship to those words, as that passage states. I cited Paul's words from Acts 17, where he told the Athenian philosophers, "*Therefore having overlooked the times of ignorance, God is now declaring to men that all everywhere should repent, because He has fixed a day in which He will judge the world in righteousness through a Man whom He has appointed, having furnished proof to all men by raising Him from the dead*" (**Acts 17:30, 31**).

The reason I cited these two passages regarding the literal future judgment was that I knew Pagitt did not believe in a literal future judgment, and I was hoping to draw him into a debate on that matter. The reason I asserted the significance and authority of God's words was that I knew he denied these ideas.

The world where God's words draw logical boundaries is not found within the worldview of the Emergent Church or of postmodern theology. Neither is facing God's wrath against sin that will climax in a literal future judgment, when all who have not repented and believed the gospel will be judged by the very Savior they have spurned. Emergent/postmodern thinkers throw these longstanding Christian beliefs into a figurative trash can labeled "modernist, Enlightenment, or foundationalist," and it is because of their rejection of the foundations that undergird human reason and communication that the Emergent Church remains a mystery to many who have worked quite hard to try to understand it.

It is impossible to have a Christian movement without categories and devoid of ideas. As successful as Emergent leaders are at communicating by way of misdirection and by being provocative without being clear, they do have some key bedrock beliefs. The most important of these is their eschatology which explains, among other things, the term "Emergent" or "Emerging."[2] In Pagitt's opening statement at our debate, he claimed to hold a "hopeful and positive view of God's engagement in the world." That hopeful view is that the kingdom of God is emerging through the processes of history because

2 There is debate whether these terms describe two movements or one. Since the intellectual leaders of the movement who write many of the books use "Emergent," I will use that term and interact with their ideas.

God *is* the future, drawing everything into Himself. They believe that God is still creating and that we can be "co-(re)creators" of the world with God.[3]

To proceed with their "conversation" that lacks boundaries but clings to hope based on a novel eschatology, they must do something with traditional Christian doctrine. Their chosen solution involves a process of "undefining" Christianity. Once again, definitions create *categories*, and categories involve *boundaries*; boundaries keep people out. The process of undefining is elaborate and somewhat heady, dealing primarily with a field of study most Christians are not trained in—epistemology (the study of *how* we know), a subject we shall examine later.

In this book I will help you to understand the Emergent Church by explaining its eschatology and showing that its very eschatology explains the rest of its beliefs and practices. To do this we must begin at the end, because knowing where they think they will end up (as well as everyone and everything else) will reveal much about the processes they believe make the emergence of a new church inevitable.

3 Doug Pagitt, *Church Re-imagined* (Grand Rapids: Zondervan, 2005 edition) 185.

Abstract Chapter 1

The Road to Paradise Imagined

COMMON THREAD - ESCHATOLOGY

While Emergent Church leaders differ on nearly every Christian doctrine, one belief they hold in common—the one that unifies their movement—is their eschatology. Emergent theologians and church leaders reject God's final judgment in favor of His saving of all of humanity and creation into a tangible paradise in which all will participate. Because everyone will participate in paradise, everyone can look with hope to the future. And because of the certainty of this wonderful future, whatever we do to make the world better is part of the actions that implement it.

DESPAIR BECOMES "HOPE"

In contrast, Francis Schaefer (1912-1984) demonstrated that "the new theology" of his day was a "theology of despair" because it denied the possibility of ever knowing the truth. People despaired because they had no hope of knowing the truth about God, about man, and about the universe. At best, their future contained only bleak uncertainty and impending judgment. Then, in the 1960s, German theologian Jürgen Moltmann, to be rid of despair, created what he called "a theology of hope" based on the philosophy of Friedrich Hegel, an 18th and 19th century progenitor of German Idealism. The Hegelian synthesis denies absolutes, such as absolute truth or knowledge, and instead claims that everything evolves as incompatible ideas merge into something new and better. Two incompatible opposites, such as good and evil, combine and evolve into an improved third option that surpasses both.

MOLTMANN EMBRACES HEGEL

Moltmann applied Hegel's synthesis to theology and eschatology, deciding that because incompatibilities were evolving into new and better things, God could not possibly allow the world to end in judgment. Instead of judgment, Moltmann set aside scripture to declare that the entire world and all of creation was heading toward paradise and progressively leaving evil behind.

1

The Road To Paradise Imagined

Imagine a world where the polarity of time is reversed so that history moves backward toward Paradise rather than forward toward judgment. Consider a world in which God is so immanently involved in the creation that He is undoing entropy[4] and recreating the world now through processes already at work. Think of a world where the future is leading to God Himself in a saving way for all people and all of creation. This imaginary world is our world viewed through the lens of Emergent eschatology.

Several acts of God's providence brought me to know the nature of Emergent theology and its unique eschatology. The first happened in 1999 during my final year in seminary when the seminary hired a new professor, LeRon Shults. Shults, a theological disciple of the German Theologian Wolfhart Pannenberg, became my professor for a logic class. Shults often described his beliefs with this simple statement: "God is the future drawing everything into Himself."

Some years later, several people suggested that I consider writing an article for *Critical Issues Commentary*, our ministry newsletter, examining a new movement called "The Emerging Church." For

4 Entropy is the principle by which physicists describe usable energy loss. The existence of entropy is a proof that the universe is not eternal because if it were infinitely old it would have already died of heat death.

my study I carefully read Brian McLaren's book *a Generous Orthodoxy*.[5] What baffled me about his theology was that his views were nearly identical to those refuted 40 years earlier by Francis Schaeffer, who had called it "the new theology." But as Schaeffer so clearly showed, the result of this theology is despair because under it there is no hope of knowing the truth. But the Emerging writers describe their theology as one of hope. If there is no hope of knowing the truth about God, man, and the universe we live in (as they claim), then how is hope the result? It turns out that a theology from the 1960s, first articulated in Germany when Schaeffer was writing his books, is the answer. We shall follow up on that idea later.

That leads to a second providential event. A member of our congregation handed me a book that she thought might be of interest in my research: *A is for Abductive – The Language of the Emerging Church*.[6] Under the entry "Eschaton," the heading "The end of entropy"[7] appears. It then says, "In the postmodern matrix there is a good chance that the world will reverse its chronological polarity for us. Instead of being bound to the past by chains of cause and effect, we will feel ourselves being pulled into the future by the magnet of God's will, God's dream, God's desire."[8] Reading this brought my mind back to 1999 and Shults' interpretation of Pannenberg: "God is the future drawing everything into Himself." Could this be the ground of Emergent "hope"?

The third providential event was the debate with Doug Pagitt, the 2006 event on the topic of The Emergent Church and Postmodern Spirituality. That event gave me the opportunity to ask Pagitt, a nationally recognized leader in the Emergent movement, whether or not he believed in a literal future judgment. He would not answer either way but did state that judgment happens now through consequences in history. His refusal to answer that question convinced me that the Pannenberg/Shults eschatology *was* behind the movement!

The fourth providential event was a meeting with Tony Jones of the Emergent Village with the goal of setting up another debate.

---

5 CIC Issue 87, March/April 2005. http://cicministry.org/commentary/issue87.htm

6 Leonard Sweet, Brian McLaren, and Jerry Haselmayer, *A is for Abductive – The Language of the Emerging Church* (Grand Rapids: Zondervan, 2003).

7 Ibid. 113.

8 Ibid.

It turned out that they did not want another debate, but Jones offered to answer any of my questions about Emergent. I responded by e-mail asking about Stanley Grenz, Wolfhart Pannenberg, LeRon Shults, and Jürgen Moltmann and their influence on Emergent theology. Jones replied that Grenz (who, as I will later show, praises the theologies of both Pannenberg and Moltmann) was influential and that Jones himself was studying under a professor named Miroslav Volf who had studied under Moltmann. Also, he helped me with his comment that their hope-filled belief generally leads them to reject eschatologies that "preach a disastrous end to the cosmos." (I appreciated Jones' willingness to show me I was looking in the right direction in my studies.)

The fifth providential event was when I fell and fractured my ankle while trimming trees. The broken ankle required that I sit with my leg elevated for a full week in order to get the swelling down. I had found a copy of Jürgen Moltmann's *Theology of Hope* that I knew I had to read if I was going to write this book and prove my thesis. Reading Moltmann was so laborious that finishing the book was not likely to be completed quickly. But because of my immobility I finished Moltmann, taking notes on the contents of every page. The same week I read Moltmann I obtained the just-published *An Emergent Manifesto of Hope* with Pagitt and Jones as the editors. I read that as well and found Moltmann cited favorably by two emergent writers.[9] In that same book Jones describes why this theology is so hopeful for them: "God's promised future is *good*, and it awaits us, beckoning us forward. We're caught in the tractor beam of redemption and re-creation, and there's no sense fighting it, so we might as well cooperate."[10] Or as professor Shults always said, "God is the future drawing everything into Himself."

All of this leads me to my thesis: That the worldview represented by the theology of Grenz, Pannenberg, Moltmann, and Shults is the bedrock foundation of the Emergent Church movement. Their language and ideas present themselves on the pages of many Emergent books. For example, McLaren writes, "In this way of seeing, God

9 In *An Emergent Manifesto of Hope* Doug Pagitt and Tony Jones editors (Grand Rapids: Baker, 2007); Moltmann is cited favorably by Dwight Friesen on page 203 and Troy Bronsink page 73 n. 24.

10 Ibid. Tony Jones, 130.

stands ahead of us in time, at the end of the journey, sending to us in waves, as it were, the gift of the present, an inrush of the future that pushes the past behind us and washes over us with a ceaseless flow of new possibilities, new options, new chances to rethink and receive new direction, new empowerment."[11] Here is Pagitt's version of it:

> God is constantly creating anew. And God also, invites us to be re-created and join the work of God as co-(re)creators. . . . Imagine the Kingdom of God as the creative process of God reengaging in all that we know and experience. . . . When we employ creativity to make this world better, we participate with God in the re-creation of the world.[12]

These writers often refer to "God's dream." Apparently they mean that God imagines an ideal future for the world that we can join and help actualize. When this dream becomes reality in the future, it will be the Kingdom of God.

This series of providential events in my life worked together to help me accurately understand a movement that works very hard to stay undefined. Definitions draw boundaries. Definitions are static. But definitions are necessary in order for us to understand anything. With no defined categories we would be hopeless human beings because, for example, we need our rational minds and valid categories to distinguish between food and poison. Definitions are valid, and no amount of philosophical legerdemain can change that reality. Definitions, to their way of thinking, impede the process of the "tractor beam" of redemption they are experiencing. They consider definitions too "foundationalist," as we will discuss in a later chapter. I believe that I can now define the Emergent Church movement more accurately because I understand what they believe.

The Emergent Church movement is an association of individuals linked by one very important, key idea: that God is bringing history toward a glorious kingdom of God on earth without future judgment. They loathe dispensationalism more than any other theol-

---

11 Brian D. McLaren, *a Generous Orthodoxy*; (Grand Rapids: Zondervan, 2004) 283.

12 Doug Pagitt, *Church Re-imagined* (Grand Rapids: Zondervan, 2003/2005) 185.

ogy because it claims just the opposite: that the world is getting ever more sinful and is sliding toward cataclysmic judgment.[13] Both of these ideas cannot be true. Either there is a literal future judgment or there is not. This is not a matter left to one's own preference.

JÜRGEN MOLTMANN

The best way to understand the Emergent theology of hope is to study its primary source: Jürgen Moltmann's 1964 book *Theology of Hope*. My copy of the book is the 1991 re-release of the book which contains a new introduction.[14] In the introduction Moltmann provides attribution for the thinking that led him to write his book: "I found important categories for the pattern of this tapestry in the messianic philosophy of the neo-Marxist Ernst Bloch."[15] Bloch was an atheist. In 1960 Moltmann read Bloch's *Principal of Hope* and proceeded to develop his idea that a Christian theology of hope would make great sense. It also would not necessarily compete against Bloch's atheist version: "The atheism that wants to free men and women from superstition and idolatry and the Christianity that wants to lead them out of inward and outward slavery into the liberty of the coming kingdom of God—these two do not have to be antagonists. They can also work together. Which of them will prove to be stronger in the long run is something we may confidently leave to the future."[16]

To most of us the idea that an atheist philosophy and Christian theology could both be valid is a contradiction. It certainly is to me. But what binds Moltmann and Bloch together is the philosophy of Georg Wilhelm Friedrich Hegel. The idea that contradictions, through the processes of history, synthesize into a better future can be found in Moltmann's theology. This is true for him because the God of hope is both coming and present, and because the world's future is also God's future. Therefore it must be a glorious future where all things are new and better. For the atheist Marxist the processes of history synthesize into a better future because it is their nature to do so.

---

13 Please note that classical amillennialism also believes that the world is facing future judgment. Emergent is not merely opposed to dispensationalism, but any version of eschatology that asserts that God will bring cataclysmic judgment at the end of the age.

14 Jürgen Moltmann, *Theology of Hope* (HarperCollins: New York, 1991).

15 Ibid. 9.

16 Ibid.

For Moltmann, the Christian and atheist can work together for that better future, and if Moltmann is right the atheist will participate in the glorious future that God brings. If the atheist is right Moltmann will participate as well (at least during this life).

It is said that Hegel is one of the most difficult philosophers to understand. It can be said that theologians who are inspired by Hegelian thinking are difficult as well. That is true of Moltmann. A survey of the index of Moltmann's book shows the following persons were the most often cited: Karl Barth on 26 pages; Rudolph Bultmann on 32 pages; and Hegel on 34 pages. He uses the three in an interesting way. He characterizes Barth's theology as "the transcendental subjectivity of God"[17] and Bultmann's as "the transcendental subjectivity of man."[18] This comes in a long section where he is seeking to establish what the idea of God's self-revelation could possibly mean. His proposed answer is a dialectic[19] synthesis of contradictions:

> This cleavage into objectification and subjectivity is not to be escaped—nor can theology escape it in bringing the gospel to the modern world—by declaring one side of this kind of thinking to be vain, deficient, corrupt and decadent. Rather, theology will have to take the hardened antitheses and make them fluid once more, to mediate in the contradiction between them and reconcile them. That, however, is only possible when the category of history, which drops out in this dualism, is rediscovered in such a way that it does not deny the antithesis in question, but spans it and understands it as an element in an advancing process.[20]

This dense theology is based on the Hegelian synthesis, as it is popularly called. And for Bloch the atheist and Moltmann the Christian

---

17 Ibid. 50 ff.

18 Ibid. 58 ff.

19 "Dialectic," as I use it and as Moltmann uses it, describes a process whereby apparently contradictory ideas are resolved into a superior but often presently unseen third option. In popular language this is described as "thesis, antithesis, and synthesis."

20 Moltmann, *Theology of Hope*, 50.

it provides the hope that future history is on course for a glorious existence.

I do not overemphasize when I say that for Moltmann, the idea of the dialectic explains almost everything in theology and history. For example, the death and resurrection of Christ are interpreted as contradiction and synthesis. (Please bear with me at this point because this material is dense and long, but necessary to address if we are to understand the Emerging Church.) Moltmann, by the way, uses the term "emerging" often in his book as characterizing that which synthesizes from contradictions:

> Only when we see the progressive, eschatological driving forces in the contradictory event of the cross and resurrection itself, do the true problems arise. The revelation—i.e. the appearances of the risen Lord—does not acquire its character of progressiveness from a reality foreign to it, from the mysteriously continuing history after Easter, but itself creates the progress in its process of contradiction to the godless reality of sin and death. It does not become progressive by 'entering into' human history; but by dint of promise, hope and criticism it makes the reality of man historic and progressive. It is the revelation of the potentiality and power of God in the raising of the one who was crucified, and the tendency and intention of God recognizable therein, that constitute the horizon of what is to be called history and to be expected as history. The revelation of God in the cross and resurrection thus sets the stage for history, on which there emerges the possibility of engulfing of all things in nothingness and of the new creation. The mission on which the man of hope is sent into this advance area of universal possibilities pursues the direction of the tendency of God's own action in omnipotently pursuing his faithfulness and his promise.[21]

21 Ibid. 226, 227.

So the cross and resurrection, seen as a dialectic, synthesize into an emerging new reality in history, and we can participate in it. I hope we all notice that this has nothing to do with the Biblical categories of the blood atonement, justification by faith, and the return of Christ to reward the righteous and judge the wicked. Such ideas are revealed in Scripture, but Moltmann does not take Scripture alone to be God's self-revelation. Rather scripture, past salvation history, and God's future are a part of a grand dialectic that is going somewhere good and hopeful.

Moltmann's view of the historical character of the resurrection of Christ is itself predicated on a dialectical understanding that synthesizes the contradictory ideas. For example, he sees a modernistic, mechanistic view of history as a "self-contained system of cause and effect"[22] that would rule out the resurrection. He contrasts that with an existential understanding of the resurrection based on the disciples' "existential decision."[23] He instead detaches the resurrection from any current views of history (or our ideas of "really happened" in a provable sense) and uses the presupposition of Christ's resurrection as the ground of a new view of history:

> Then the theology of the resurrection would no longer be fitted in with an existing concept of history, but an attempt would have to be made, in comparison with and contradistinction to the existing views of history, to arrive at a new understanding of history with the ultimate possibilities and hopes that attach to it on the presupposition of the raising of Christ from the dead.[24]

But if we cannot know Christ was raised by any ordinary way of knowing the truth of historical events, how do we know that the presupposition of such a resurrection is a better one than, say, a presupposition that Joseph Smith really had the definitive revelation of God?

For Moltmann this presupposition is the ground of belief that God is still creatively involved in the processes of history leading them to a glorious future:

22 Ibid. 177.
23 Ibid. 178.
24 Ibid. 180.

> The raising of Christ is then to be called 'historic', not because it took place *in* history to which other categories of some sort provide a key, but it is to be called historic because, by pointing the way for future events, it *makes* history in which we can and must live. It is historic, because it discloses an eschatological future. This assertion must then give proof of itself in conflict with other concepts of history, all of which are ultimately based on other 'history-making' events, shocks, or revolutions in history.[25]

But as Moltmann's reader I'm nearly persuaded to scream, "Was Jesus really bodily raised from the dead, and did He appear bodily to reliable witnesses, and must I believe in the saving value of His death, burial, and resurrection in order to be saved from God's wrath?" His answer is that we cannot expect to know these matters because the proof of what type of world or history lies in the future, where God is bringing history. So, as he said earlier, that might be the future as understood by atheistic Marxists. If so, we shall find out. According to this view, our hope is not in Jesus' resurrection that furnished proof to all men and thus made them accountable (as Paul said in Acts 17:31), but in Jesus' resurrection as a view of history with a hopeful future.

As we shall see with the Emergent Church's theology, which is derived from Moltmann and others, a serious problem exists. The problem is that this hope is based on an the idea that history is not headed toward cataclysmic judgment in which those who do not believe the Christian gospel are judged and lost for eternity but is headed toward the kingdom of God on earth with universal participation. But what if Paul was right and the resurrection of Christ means judgment for all who refused the "proof" it provided? With the Moltmann and Emergent idea, we cannot know what is "true" about competing religious ideas until the future, at which time God brings things to where He is drawing them. For most people it will be too late! We cannot expect to stand before God's judgment seat and then say, "Okay, now I see which view of history was correct; let me into the kingdom."

25 Ibid. 181 emphasis in original.

Moltmann's understanding of the resurrection of Christ is so obscure that pages and pages of dense writing are required just to determine what it means to refer to the event as "historical." Hegelian synthesis supposedly helps us find this meaning in the future—a future that is projected to be a good one. But this means that apocalyptic visions of future cataclysm caused by God's wrath cannot be the Biblical message. Therefore he rejects the "apocalyptic" idea that God will judge evil and set up a world of righteousness populated by believers. Moltmann writes:

> The apocalyptic expectation is no longer directed toward a consummation of the creation through the overcoming of evil by good, but towards the separation of good and evil and hence replacement of the 'world that lies under the power of evil' by the coming 'world of righteousness'. This shows a fatalistic dualism which is not yet so found in the prophets.[26]

What he means by the overcoming of evil by good is that this happens beyond history (what he calls "Christ's future") and not by any cataclysmic judgment of the wicked who eventually end up in the lake of fire. That would be "fatalistic dualism" to his way of thinking. In contrast, heaven and hell, if they literally exist, are not subject to a dialectic process that ends up with a better future universally for all people. Some come under eternal judgment.

Moltmann's theology, which embraces the Hegelian dialectic and uses it to interpret Christian hope, comes from philosophy, not careful Biblical interpretation. He feels no need to deal with passages of Scripture that contradict his ideas, but this is not surprising coming from a 20th-century German theologian. In the German theological schools, theology and philosophy had often been so intertwined that they were inseparable. This happened when the Bible ceased to be considered God's inerrant, verbal, self-revelation. If the Bible were considered inerrant, then its statements about heaven and hell, future judgment, the terms of justification, and everything else would define

26 Ibid. 134.

truth. But for Moltmann and his 21st-century Emergent followers, the Bible is not viewed as such.

CONTEMPORARY DISCIPLES OF MOLTMANN

Typically Emergent writers exhibit either thinking like Moltmann or the thinking of Moltmann. To demonstrate this I will cite some examples from the previously mentioned *An Emergent Manifesto of Hope*. Barry Taylor, who teaches at Fuller Theological Seminary, begins his essay with this paradox: "God is nowhere. God is now here."[27] What does this paradox mean? It means that we are to jettison historical concepts of God: "Faith in the twenty-first century is not exclusively centered on concepts of God."[28] He repeats "God is nowhere, God is now here" a half dozen times. Taylor analyzes the idea of God's death similar to the way Hegel does as cited by Moltmann. Writes Taylor, "We live in a post-Neitzschean world of faith and spirituality. Nietzsche's declaration that God is dead still holds true, since interest in all things spiritual does not necessarily translate to a belief in a metaphysical God or the tenets and dogmas of a particular faith."[29] Compare what Moltmann wrote: "Hegel in 1802 described the 'death of God' as the basic feeling of the religion of modern times . . ."[30] That was before Nietzsche's birth. Moltmann then cites Hegel and addresses how Hegel's ideas could be used to interpret Good Friday and resurrection through a dialectical process that would deliver us from both "romanticist nihilism" and "the metholodical [sic] atheism of science" to a synthetic, hopeful future.[31] We can see the same thinking in Taylor: "*God is nowhere. God is now here.* God is present; God is absent. The future of faith rests in the tension between these words, and it is from this place of discomfort and complexity that new life emerges."[32] This, too, coincides with Hegel's ideas.

27 Barry Taylor, "Converting Christianity The End and Beginning of Faith," in *Emergent Manifesto of Hope* 164.
28 Ibid. 165
29 Ibid.
30 Moltmann, *Theology of Hope,* 168.
31 Moltmann, 169.
32 Taylor, 170.

Another Emergent author, Dwight J. Friesen, is such a proponent of Moltmann's theological use of Hegelian thinking that he entitled his essay "Orthoparadoxy - Emerging Hope for Embracing Difference."[33] Friesen praises Moltmann's *Theology of Hope* as a "ground breaking book" and cites it approvingly in regard to contradictions containing possibilities and hope for the future.[34] Friesen writes, "Just as he [Moltmann] highlights the necessity of contradictions for life, so I declare that embracing the complexities of contradictions, antinomies, and paradoxes of the human life is walking in the way of Jesus."[35] In keeping with Moltmann's theology and Emergent thinking in general, Friesen sees the process of embracing contradiction as leading to the kingdom of God becoming "manifest" in the world: "An orthoparadox ethic rightly holds differences, tensions, and paradoxes in reconciling movement toward oneness with the other. When orthorparadoxy becomes our way of being in the world, the kingdom of God is manifest."[36]

Lost in this perspective is any hope of actually knowing something to be truth that will continue to be true forever and binding upon those who will one day appear before God in judgment. Friesen says, "Othoparadox theology is less concerned with creating 'once for all' doctrinal statements or dogmatic claims and is more interested in holding competing truth claims in right tension."[37] As with Moltmann, Friesen never addresses clear Bible statements that refute Friesen's claims. Jude told us to "earnestly contend for the faith once for all delivered to the saints." The Biblical writers did not see this once-for-all delivered faith as a grand jumble of contradictions and paradoxes.

A paradox, by the way, is meaningless, like a square circle. One can say the words "square circle" but cannot contemplate the meaning of the statement. Jesus did not think His words were contradictory or paradoxical: "*He who rejects Me, and does not receive My sayings, has one who judges him; the word I spoke is what will judge him at the last day*" (**John 12:48**). This one statement by Jesus challenges Emergent theology to

---

33 Dwight J. Friesen, "Orthoparadoxy Emerging Hope for Embracing Difference," in *Emergent Manifesto of Hope*, 201 - 212.

34 Ibid. 203.

35 Ibid.

36 Ibid. 206.

37 Ibid. 209

its very core. Jesus spoke words, these words conveyed binding truth, once for all, and are so authoritative that for those who reject them they shall serve as condemning evidence against them at God's future judgment. This is no dialectic process but truth spoken for all people telling them to either believe and be saved or reject and be lost.

Another influential theologian in the Emergent movement and postmodern theology in general is the late Stanley Grenz. Grenz's book *Beyond Foundationalism – Shaping Theology in a Postmodern Context* (coauthored by John R. Franke) shows how the ideas of Pannenberg and Moltmann are being fleshed out in America at the beginning of the 21st century.[38] Grenz quotes Moltmann extensively and positively, quite accurately explaining his theology, even down to acknowledging its Marxist roots.[39] Grenz makes the caveat that he is concerned that Moltmann's interpretation of Bloch is in danger of "slipping into an anthropocentric foundationalism, which replaces the specificity of the biblical hope for hope as a structure of human existence."[40] Inasmuch as Moltmann did say that the Marxist version is not in competition with his, Grenz is correct to be concerned about that. But what is amazing is that he claims that we want to embrace the "specificity of the biblical hope" when I do not see Grenz doing so himself! I say that because a literal future judgment in which some are raised to eternal life and others are raised and consigned to the lake of fire is as absent from Grenz's theology as it is from Moltmann's.

One reason for the absence of the specifics of God's future promises according to Grenz's eschatology is his practice (mentioned earlier) of feeling free to ignore whatever Biblical material doesn't suit his purposes. For example, here is a passage Paul wrote to persecuted Christians that describe a specific Christian hope:

> *This is a plain indication of God's righteous judgment so that you may be considered worthy of the kingdom of God, for which indeed you are suffering. For after all it is only just for God to repay with affliction those who afflict you, and to give relief to you who are afflicted and to us as well when the Lord*

38 Stanley Grenz and John R. Franke, *Beyond Foundationalism – Shaping Theology in a Postmodern Context* (Louisville: Westminster John Knox Press, 2001).

39 Ibid. 247.

40 Ibid.

> *Jesus shall be revealed from heaven with His mighty angels in flaming fire, dealing out retribution to those who do not know God and to those who do not obey the gospel of our Lord Jesus. And these will pay the penalty of eternal destruction, away from the presence of the Lord and from the glory of His power, when He comes to be glorified in His saints on that day, and to be marveled at among all who have believed--for our testimony to you was believed.* (**2Thessalonians 1:5-10**)

Laying aside all the sophistry that Grenz has used to undermine the possibility that we actually can know with clarity what the Bible means, this passage is not that hard to understand. There will be a future judgment, and the future is not universally an ideal future for all people regardless of their present beliefs and actions. Paul taught it, and no one can deny it. The only thing left for Moltmann, Grenz, and their Emergent followers is to deny that we can know what the Bible means. I will deal with their method in another chapter. But know that when they are talking about "Christian hope" they are not using the same categories of thought as those of the Biblical writers.

This section from a chapter entitled "Eschatology: Theology's Orienting Motif" shows how divergent the eschatology of Grenz and his co-author is from specific Biblical promises about the end of the age. Consider this:

> There is a real universe "out there," we readily acknowledge. But this reality–this "out there"–lies "before," rather than "beneath" or "around" us. Ours is a universe that is in the process of being created, as many scientists acknowledge [a book about theology in an evolutionary world is cited]. Therefore, rather than merely being discovered via experimentation, the new creation toward which our world is developing is experienced through anticipation. . . . As God's image bearers, we have a divinely given mandate to participate in God's work of constructing a world in

> the present that reflects God's own eschatological will for creation.[41]

He goes on, based on the idea of socially constructed reality and linguistics, to explain how we participate with God constructing the future world God intends. For example, "We participate with God, for through the constructive power of language we inhabit a present linguistic world that sees all reality from the perspective of the future, real world that God is bringing to pass."[42] But this future world cannot now be known, according to Grenz's understanding, because it is not objective until the future. This postmodern thinking denies the objectivity of historic knowledge, denies the objectivity of present knowledge, but asserts the objectivity of future knowledge. Grenz writes, "Therefore, the 'objectivity of the world' about which we can truly speak is an objectivity of a *future*, eschatological world."[43]

So in this view, we now live in a socially constructed, linguistic reality that is not objectively known. The "real" world is the future world; the words of the Bible do not authoritatively and objectively tell us the details of the future world; and God is immanently involved in the present world creating and causing it to move toward the future world. In this view we are to participate in God's work of creating the future world but we have no objective knowledge of what this future world is—*yet*. Moltmann, Grenz, and the Emergent Church tell us that this constitutes "hope."

I must say that I cannot see how that lack of objective knowledge about the currently unknowable future should be construed as "hope." This concept holds only if they are right that the world is growing toward the kingdom and there is no future judgment. If this future world is different than they (in neglect of the Biblical data about future judgment) deem it to be, they may be no more than romantics looking at life through rose-colored glasses. Grenz says, "Through the use of linguistic models and under the guidance of the Holy Spirit, the Christian community constructs a particular world for human habitation. . . . In short, then, theologians assist the church in the

41 Ibid. 272.

42 Ibid.

43 Ibid. emphasis in original.

world-construction business we share."[44] In my assessment, this hope, though said to be hope in God, is really hope in man.

The Bible says that God spoke and the world that we live in came into being. It says that it was marred by the Fall and faces judgment. The theology that spawned the Emergent Church says that we construct the world into a better future with God's help, as co-(re) creators of the world with God (using Pagitt's terminology). There are various ways they see this happening. Moltmann laid great stress on the Hegelian dialectic. Grenz stresses socially constructed reality and linguistics for creating the future world. Contemporary Emergent writers stress various versions of good works, the social gospel, and cooperation with other religions to bring the future kingdom of God to pass. But all agree that the future is glorious, hopeful, universally good news for all people and the creation itself, and they deny that a cataclysmic, cosmic, judgment will occur which will permanently separate good from evil. Emergent leaders see a glorious journey toward paradise, not the threat of divine judgment. But what if they are wrong?

In summary, the "hope" of Emergent/postmodern theology is based on the Hegelian idea that contradictions synthesize into better future realities. Hegel's ideas are philosophical and have not been proven in the real world. Moltmann took Hegel's ideas and created a Christian alternative to Marxism (which is also based on Hegel's philosophy) that he called a "theology of hope." Emergent Church leaders published a book entitled *An Emergent Manifesto of Hope* that cites and echoes Moltmann's ideas. A key book on postmodern theology by Grenz does the same. The "hope" espoused by these teachers is not based on literal promises found in the Bible, but rather on philosophical speculation. In the last chapter of this book I will return to this idea and discuss the ideas of the contemporary philosopher Ken Wilber, which also are based on Hegel and have strongly influenced Emergent teachers.

In the next chapter we will examine what the Emergent Church means when it says they are "missional." We will see that they doubt that truth about rigid theological categories can be known, but are certain they can know the nature of the Christian mission.

---

44 Ibid. 273.

Abstract Chapter 2

Undefining God's Mission - The Emerging Church "On a Mission from God"

MISSIONARY OR MISSIONAL?

For hundreds, if not thousands, of years Christians have used the term "missionary" to describe one who goes out to preach the gospel to an unsaved world headed toward judgment–repentance for the forgiveness of sin found in the death and resurrection of Christ. The mission of the missionary was to proclaim the absolute truth of the gospel–a fact proven by Jesus' resurrection from the dead. The gospel is "good news" because it provides condemned sinners with a certain escape from God's wrath.

MISSIONAL MEANS ZEALOUS–ABOUT WHAT?

Emergent's word "missional" *does not* convey this meaning. "Missional" sounds like "missionary" except that the "mission" is undefined. Emergent leaders disagree among themselves concerning the definition of their "mission," but the mission they tend to embrace is to improve society now. They borrow much from Catholic liberation theologians and liberalism itself–that Christianity's mission is to make the world a tangible paradise immediately. Outside of bettering society, the missional concept has no content; it specifically denies a mission of proclaiming an escape from God's coming wrath. For Emergent, "The journey *is* the reward," and the journey will certainly end well for all–without exception. According to Emergent thinking, being missional means following the journey wherever it leads as long as it corrects society's evils. In their view, missional is more like the opposite of apathy; it is zeal to right the wrongs of society. Because the eschatological end of the journey is assured for everyone, the path the journey takes doesn't matter much. One mission to fight social evil is as good as another; what matters most is that we are missional together.

"ESCAPE FROM COMING WRATH" OR A "CERTAIN FUTURE OF HOPE"

The content of the gospel (that God has offered a path to escape His coming wrath) is the core issue to a missionary but irrelevant to one who is missional. To the missionary, those who repent and believe the gospel are reconciled to God and enter His kingdom. That message is unimportant, or at least not central, to one who is missional. Why? Because to the Emergent there is no impending judgment and if we do something nice on our journey nothing more is needed. To them, a focus on the content of the message is a distraction at best and harmful at worst.

2

Undefining God's Mission - The Emergent Church "On a Mission from God"

Almost universally, people involved with the Emergent "conversation" espouse one theme: they consider themselves to be missional. Being "missional" is not what traditional Christians have known as "missions." We have believed that the Christian mission was to send people with the message of the gospel to places where the gospel had not been heard—to preach it and establish churches. As Christianity became established in various cultures, other Christian workers usually came to establish schools, hospitals, and perform other practical expressions of Christian love and mercy. This is not what Emergent thinkers have in mind when they describe themselves as "missional."

For one thing, the description above started with the idea of the gospel as defined in the Bible. The Emergent mission does not begin with any theological idea. It is not gleaned from Biblical texts such as this one: "*and that repentance for forgiveness of sins should be proclaimed in His name to all the nations, beginning from Jerusalem*" (**Luke 24:47**). In fact the Emergent mission does not even start from a set of theological beliefs. I say this because their use of "missional" describes the idea that any works that make the world a better place bring us toward the ideal future.

As we saw in the previous chapter, the Hegelian synthesis is ever lurking in the background of Emergent thinking; and this is the case with the idea of "missional." For example, Brian McLaren writes concerning his idea of "missional:" "The term, as I understand it, attempts to find a generous third way beyond the conservative and liberal versions of Christianity so dominant in the Western world."[45] McLaren's idea is that one does not begin with a set of theological beliefs that determine one's mission, but rather begins with a mission and some sort of theology emerges in the process: "Theology is the church on a mission reflecting on its message, its identity, its meaning."[46] So in his thinking we can know our mission before we know theological truth.

When I first read that I thought it irrational on the grounds that one would need some theological belief in order to justify going on any mission in God's name. Our *a priori* beliefs tell us what an appropriate mission would be. That was before I discovered their eschatological beliefs. Now I know why they are missional. They believe God to be bringing everything along toward an ideal future without judgment. Therefore any practice deemed to make the world better is a suitable mission. In their view the only thing that *doesn't* make sense is preaching repentance for the forgiveness of sins so people can avoid a literal, future judgment (because they do not believe in future judgment). Ironically, the one approach to missions that Emergent leaders reject routinely is the one based on Jesus' own words to His church.

Not surprisingly, Jürgen Moltmann, 40 years ago, proposed that in light of his eschatology, what we have *now* is a mission—the knowledge of truth is something that lies in the future.[47] For example, Motlmann writes, "The horizon within which the resurrection of Christ becomes knowable as 'resurrection', is the horizon of promise and mission, beckoning us on to his future and the future of his lordship."[48] Moltmann claims that we cannot even know what "resurrection" means or even what the resurrection of Christ means until the future:

---

45 Brian McLaren, *a Generous Orthodoxy* (El Cajon, CA: Youth Specialties, 2004; published by Zondervan) 105.

46 Ibid.

47 Jürgen Moltmann, *Theology of Hope* (New York: HarperCollins, 1991) 194 - 197.

48 Ibid. 196.

> 'Raising of the dead' is an expression which looks expectantly towards the future proof of God's creative power over the non-existent. What 'resurrection of the dead' really is, and what 'actually happened' in the raising of Jesus, is thus a thing which not even the New Testament Easter narratives profess to know. From the two mutually radically contradictory experiences of the cross and the appearances of Jesus, they argue to the event in between as an eschatological event for which the verifying analogy is as yet only in prospect and is still to come.[49]

So in this thinking we really do not know what the cross or the resurrection of Christ mean since they are deemed "contradictory," but we will find out in the future. Yet we continue to have a mission. The only reason by which a Christian mission is deemed valid is a dialectic process that leads somewhere universally good. Moltmann states, "Cross and resurrection are then not merely *modi* in the person of Christ. Rather, their dialectic is an open dialectic, which will find its resolving synthesis only in the *eschaton* of all things.[50]

Knowing that Moltmann's theology (and that of others similar to his) lies at the heart of the many Emergent leaders' thinking, let us think again about McLaren's previously cited statement: "Theology is the church on a mission reflecting on its message, its identity, its meaning." The reason he thinks we do not know these things now, is that according to the Emergent eschatology they are by nature *unknowable* (now, that is). So the only recourse is to discover one's mission in the world through observation, with the belief that the many contradictions that one encounters are being synthesized into a new, better reality that lies in the future. This is very much what Moltmann himself stated:

> The Christian consciousness of history is not a consciousness of the millennia of all history, in some mysterious knowledge of a divine plan for history, but is a missionary consciousness in the knowledge of a divine

49 Ibid. 197.

50 Ibid. 201. "eschaton" means the end or final destiny of things; emphasis in original.

> commission, and is therefore a consciousness of the contradiction inherent in this unredeemed world, and the sign of the cross under which the Christian mission and the Christian hope stand."[51]

In other words we have no knowledge of a divine commission, and, as I cited him earlier, we have no knowledge of what the cross and resurrection mean, either (at least not now). So we have an undefined mission that must be discovered.

McLaren and others are quite sure of the one thing the mission is *not*: the salvation of souls so that people go to heaven when they die. He and other Emergent writers regularly mock that idea as a consumer good being sold to the unsuspecting for the benefit of badly motivated religious leaders. For example, McLaren writes, "Is it any surprise that it's stinking hard to convince churches that they have a mission to the world when most Christians equate 'personal salvation' of individual 'souls' with the ultimate aim of Jesus? Is it any wonder that people feel like victims of a bait and switch when they're lured with personal salvation and then hooked with church commitment and world mission?"[52] The only reason McLaren thinks ideas such as salvation from God's future judgment are unworthy of defining the church's mission is because he does not believe in a literal future judgment. And as we saw in the previous chapter he and his co-authors of another book think we are headed toward a universal paradise. Rescuing perishing souls when no one's soul is actually going to perish is certainly a fool's mission—unless, of course, the Bible is true, and there *is* a literal hell and many people will end up there!

GAINING THEOLOGY BY OBSERVING PAGANS

Brian McLaren credits Vincent Donavan, a Roman Catholic missionary, as a key figure who inspired him to change his ideas about the meaning of salvation and the Christian mission.[53] He cites Donovan to support his claim that one's mission is not to be found in a prior theological understanding:

---

51 Ibid. 195.

52 McLaren, *Generous*, 107.

53 Ibid. 91-93.

> I was to learn that any theology or theory that makes no reference to previous missionary experience, which does not take that experience into account, is a dead and useless thing . . . praxis must be prior to theology . . . In my work [theology would have to proceed] from practice to theory. If a theology did emerge from my work, it would have to be a theology growing out of the life and experience of the pagan peoples of the savannahs of East Africa.[54]

This means that apparently having been given no clear instructions from Jesus Christ, the true Head of the Church, about what He wants us to do and teach, we gain a theology by observing the pagans. Furthermore, we have to allow practice to hold priority over belief.

Let us consider several ramifications of this "missional" thinking of the Emergent Church. First, rather than learning about God and His will from special revelation (the Bible) we must learn about Him from general revelation (observation of creation). The term "theology" means the study of God. General revelation shows us that there is a Creator (see Romans 1 and Psalm 19), but the knowledge gained through general revelation is not a saving knowledge–it is a condemning knowledge, according to Paul's teaching in Romans 1. Saving knowledge comes through special revelation:

> *God, after He spoke long ago to the fathers in the prophets in many portions and in many ways, in these last days has spoken to us in His Son, whom He appointed heir of all things, through whom also He made the world. . . . How shall we escape if we neglect so great a salvation? After it was at the first spoken through the Lord, it was confirmed to us by those who heard,* (**Hebrews 1:1, 2** and **2:3**)

The only knowledge of God the pagans have is through general revelation. This leads to all manner of pagan religions and wicked practices. Pagan religious practices are notoriously abusive. That being the case, how does one construct a theology from observation of pagans in the

54 Vincent Donovan cited by McLaren, *Generous* 92.

mission field? Had God not chosen to reveal Himself through His spoken words and the person and work of Christ, the whole world would be pagan and devoted to various versions of nature worship or creature worship. Observing creation or human cultures devoid of the gospel cannot produce a valid theology.

Second, the notion that one's practice must hold priority over theology (a claim constantly repeated by Emergent authors) is equally invalid. What people believe will determine what practices they value. Any study of world religions makes that clear. The caste system in India, pagan child sacrifice, the traditional Islamic treatment of women, and other practices are driven by theological ideas. If Emergent followers claim they are going to do good to all people and make the world a better place, they must have some source for their definition of what is a "good" practice as opposed to what is a bad one. If the source is the "red letters" of the Bible, as some claim, then they do have a theology that is prior to their praxis. They, for some reason, have determined that some of Jesus' teachings are ethically good and worthy to guide their practice. But the "red letters" were not found on the pagan mission field; they were found in the Holy Spirit-inspired Bible. They must have some *a priori* theology about Jesus that would cause them to think His ethical teachings are superior to the teachings of Hinduism that resulted in the idea of karma and the caste system.

Third, if indeed the missional approach that knows very little about theology, while being quite certain that one's mission is valid, it is incumbent upon those so certain about their mission to validate it in some manner that is not self-referential. For example, claiming to be on a mission from God without any possible way of knowing what God has said is a self-validating claim. How do they know any mission is a God-selected mission for them? "Because God is good and of course God wants us to do good rather than evil." How then do they know their definition of "good" is the same as God's? If they keep pressing the question they are forced to accept some sort of communication from God. If such communication exists and is valid, then God has spoken. If God has spoken, then we can know the truth about Him and His will. If we know the truth about Him and His will from valid, verbal communication, then we can know what mission He wants us on. If we know that, the "missional" claims of the Emergent Church are false. If we cannot know that, then why go to a pagan people and try to persuade them to stop putting their young girls in temples to be abused by priests? Maybe their gods really told them to do that and are pleased with the practice.

This underscores a huge flaw in the teachings of the Emergent Church. If we cannot know the truth about anything with certainty until the future, then we really cannot know what our mission is either. The only way we can know what the future holds is if God has revealed it through infallible prophets. But what He has revealed through infallible prophets is rejected by Emergent writers because they cannot tolerate a scenario in which the cosmos comes to a violent end, as described in Scripture:

> *But the day of the Lord will come like a thief, in which the heavens will pass away with a roar and the elements will be destroyed with intense heat, and the earth and its works will be burned up. Since all these things are to be destroyed in this way, what sort of people ought you to be in holy conduct and godliness, looking for and hastening the coming of the day of God, on account of which the heavens will be destroyed by burning, and the elements will melt with intense heat!* (**2Peter 3:10 – 12**)

If they feel free to reject the teachings of the Bible on the grounds that no one is sure what the Bible means (a claim we shall address in a later chapter), they have therefore cut themselves off from any means of knowing the future with certainty.

So for them, like Moltmann, the truth will only be known with certainty in the future. Once again, if the *truth* cannot be known about the future *until* the future, then a valid mission cannot be known either. Mission, by its very nature, is an attempt to serve God by doing His will in order to further His purposes for the church in the world. But if they have no idea that their understanding of God's ultimate will for all is any better than the ideas held by those of different religions, they cannot know that their missional calling as they understand it is not *fighting against* what God wills to happen. They have gone willingly into a hopeless quagmire of unknowing.

But theirs is a theology of "hope." They evidently believe that Peter was dead wrong when he predicted the demise of the earth in a future conflagration of God's judgment. They rather believe that God is re-creating the world now with our help. So the mission has to be defined in terms of making the world a better place for all. Brian McLaren is a Christian, he says, because he believes God is saving the world, and that means "planet Earth and all life on it."[55] In a backward chain of reasoning, the pagan world determines their practice; their practice determines their theology; and their theology is one of hope because they decided it is the one they like best because it states that the world has a universally bright future with no pending, cataclysmic judgment.

THE "SECRET" MESSAGE AS KNOWN BY BRIAN MCLAREN

In a monograph by that title, McLaren claims to have discovered "The Secret Message of Jesus."[56] In an endnote to chapter one McLaren reveals the subtitle he wished to have used, but did not in order to avoid being "ungainly." The subtitle could have been, "*The Secret Message of Jesus: His surprising and Largely Untried Plan for a Political, Social, Religious, Artistic, Economic, Intellectual, and Spiritual Revolution.*"[57] The plan McLaren discovered through a supposedly astute reading of the gospels is a plan to establish the Kingdom of God now through the social gospel. McLaren asks:

> What if Jesus' secret message reveals a secret plan? What if he didn't come to start a new religion–but rather came to start a political, social, religious, artistic, economic, intellectual, and spiritual revolution that would give birth to a new world?[58]

In his subtle fashion he suggests the new world order that Jesus supposedly envisioned that was supposed to happen through processes within history.

According to McLaren's reading of the gospels, the church got it wrong. It historically understood that it was supposed to preach the gospel, which would rescue people from God's wrath against their sin through application of the blood atonement. But finally–after all these

55 McLaren, *Generous*, 97.

56 Brian McLaren, *The Secret Message of Jesus – Uncovering the Truth That Could Change Everything* (Nashville: W Publishing Group, 2006).

57 Ibid. 229 n. 1.

58 Ibid. 4.

years—finally Jesus' message is understood by a select few who are better readers than those who have gone before.[59] They have discovered that Jesus never intended that we warn people about how to escape future judgment and how to receive the gift of eternal life so they will join Him when they die. He never intended for us to think we needed Him to do something for us in order to avoid going to hell. He actually was hoping we would go to work to help God fulfill His dreams of a better world. McLaren explains:

> And more still . . . these words [McLaren's rejection of God's future judgment of the world through cataclysmic destruction] make me happy for God. Like a mother dreaming of a good future for the baby at her breast, like a father standing at the crib watching his newborn sleep peacefully, God will see God's own primal dream for creation finally coming true—and that dream won't be imposed by God from outside by domination against creation's will, but it will emerge from within creation itself, so that God's dream and creation's groaning for fulfillment are one.[60]

That statement gives us a good idea what "emerging" is all about for the Emergent Church. God is doing something in creation that will cause paradise to emerge within time without the type of judgment stated in Scripture and understood by most Christians throughout the Church age. It is not hard to see the theology of Moltmann here, and as we will see later, the philosophy of Ken Wilber.

McLaren's hopeful eschatology is the only thing, in my opinion, that separates the rest of *The Secret Message of Jesus* from the old-fashioned social gospel of theological liberalism. As I read his book I found the social gospel on nearly every page. When people practice the social gospel (working to make the world a better place by promoting and practicing ideas common to both theological and political liberalism) they supposedly help God's "dreams" come true. This idea of helping God solve the

59 McLaren cites his English majors in college and graduate school that gave him "sensitivities" to read the parables and thus find the secret message. Ibid. 43.

60 Ibid. 202-203.

world's problems has been promoted by various streams of liberalism for more than a century. The difference for Moltmann and McLaren is that they claim to know that we will succeed in making it happen.

McLaren's terminology (which strikes me as a textbook example of misused anthropomorphism) reveals a very shoddy understanding of God's sovereign power over His own universe: "Perhaps all along, my deepest joy has never been to have all my dreams come true, but rather to have God's one dream come true: *that this world will become a place God is at home in, a place God takes pride and pleasure in, a place where God's dreams come true.*"[61] So the missional, Emergent "follower of Jesus" is on a mission to help God have his dreams come true. The term "dreams" as McLaren uses it for himself and God means "one's hope for an ideal future."[62] This is a stark departure from a theology of God grounded in the teachings of Scripture.

Let us consider some Biblical passages at this point and then contemplate the claim that God has dreams for the future in much the same way we do. For example, "*Remember the former things long past, For I am God, and there is no other; I am God, and there is no one like Me, declaring the end from the beginning And from ancient times things which have not been done, Saying, 'My purpose will be established, And I will accomplish all My good pleasure'*" (**Isaiah 46:9, 10**). This hardly gives us the impression that God needs our help or has dreams somehow contingent upon things outside of Himself or beyond His control. Paul taught: "*also we have obtained an inheritance, having been predestined according to His purpose who works all things after the counsel of His will*" (**Ephesians 1:11**). The following passage from Psalms reveals truth about God and His relationship to His own creation that is far different from McLaren's:

> *Forever, O Lord, Your word is settled in heaven. Your faithfulness continues throughout all generations; You established the earth, and it stands. They stand this day according to Your ordinances, For* ***all things are Your servants***. (**Psalm 119:89 – 91**)

61 Ibid. 203 emphasis in original.

62 Ibid. 142. I say that because McLaren states that his "dream of God" idea is that "evoked by Dr. Martin Luther King." When King said, "I have a dream" he was explaining his hope for an ideal future that would be brought to pass through processes within history.

Consider this passage: "*But our God is in the heavens; He does whatever He pleases*" (**Psalm 115:3**). God neither dreams in the manner that humans do nor does He have to wait 2000 years hoping that His own church will finally, for the first time, find out that Jesus really meant to teach us the social gospel so we could turn this world into the kingdom of God through good works. According to the Bible, God speaks, God decrees, and God brings to pass. *He does not dream about a possible, contingent future!*

As I continue to read the literature being published by the leaders of the Emergent Church it becomes clear to me why they have so much disdain for systematic theology. What we just saw in comparing McLaren's teaching on God's "dreams" and Biblical material about God's sovereign decrees is a good case in point. If McLaren were forced to be "systematic" in his use of Scripture he would be required to deal with passages like those I cited. But he does not. He tells us how he reads the gospels and what he has gleaned, but he sees no need to give account for any other material in the Bible even though other passages contradict to his own teachings. That is how he is able to sustain his social gospel–by neglect of the whole counsel of God.

This same dynamic applies to McLaren's definition of the kingdom of God. He says, "Interestingly, John almost never uses the term 'kingdom of God' (which is at the heart of Jesus' message for Matthew, Mark and Luke)."[63] But when John does use the term he teaches things that do not fit McLaren's theological grid. John's Gospel cites Jesus teaching that one must be "born again" to see the Kingdom and enter it (John 3:3-5). John's gospel also features this statement by Jesus: "*Jesus answered, 'My kingdom is not of this world. If My kingdom were of this world, then My servants would be fighting, that I might not be delivered up to the Jews; but as it is, My kingdom is not of this realm.'*" (**John 18:36**). What John does write about the kingdom of God disproves McLaren's teachings about it. The kingdom is not of this world, and only those supernaturally born again may enter it.

But McLaren diverts his readers from what John actually wrote, and instead does some creative reinterpretation of the idea of "eternal life" in John's gospel. McLaren states, "Unfortunately the phrase *eternal life* is often misinterpreted to mean 'life in heaven after you die"–as are

63 Ibid. 36.

kingdom of God and its synonym, *kingdom of heaven*—so I think we need to find a better rendering."[64] Here is his better rendering:

> Near the end of John's account, Jesus makes a particularly fascinating statement in a prayer, and it is as close as we get to a definition: "This is eternal life: that they may know you, the only true God, and Jesus Christ whom [God has] sent." (John 17:3). So here, "eternal life" means knowing, and knowing means an interactive relationship. In other words, "This is eternal life, to have an interactive relationship with the only true God and with Jesus Christ, his messenger." Interestingly, that's what a kingdom is too: an interactive relationship one has with a king, the king's other subjects, and so on.[65]

In a footnote, McLaren credits the Christian mystic Dallas Willard for the terminology "interactive relationship."[66] McLaren's interpretation of John 17:3 is suspect.

The real point is that those who know God through Christ are the ones who have received the gift of eternal life. John does not define "know God" as "interactive relationship." The topic of eternal life was taken up extensively in John 3, where the Kingdom of God is mentioned. The issues revealed in John 3 have to do with being born again and believing so as not to perish. (To perish meant to abide under God's judgment. See John 3:1-15.) McLaren obscures John's gospel in order to import his own definition of the kingdom (which, according to McLaren, is very much of this world or realm).

Furthermore the idea of going to heaven is indeed found in John. In John 3:13-15 Jesus is the one who ascends into heaven and is the one who gives eternal life. Here is what Jesus said to his disciples who believed Him:

> *Do not let your heart be troubled; believe in God, believe also in Me. In My Father's house are many dwelling places; if it were not so, I would have told you; for I go to prepare a place*

---

64 Ibid.

65 Ibid. 37.

66 I deal with Willard's theology in *CIC* Issue 91; November/December 2005.

> *for you. If I go and prepare a place for you, I will come again and receive you to Myself, that where I am, there you may be also.* (**John 14:1-3**)

Where exactly is this "Father's house" to which Jesus will bring believers? Jesus said in verse 12, "I go to the Father." McLaren ignores John's most pertinent passages on the matter of the kingdom of God, and his meaning of having eternal life. McLaren cites a passage not pertinent to the concept of the kingdom of God and misuses it to redefine what Jesus means by "knowing God." He misinterprets John to be teaching McLaren's own version of the social gospel as "the kingdom of God." This is a flawed approach to reading any literature, much less God's inspired Scriptures.

Here is the result of McLaren's rendition of John's gospel:

> So John's related phrases–*eternal life, life to the full,* and simply *life*–give us a unique angle on what Jesus meant by "kingdom of God": a life that is radically different from the way people are living these days, a life that is full and over-flowing, a higher life that is centered in an interactive relationship with God and with Jesus. Let's render it simply 'an extraordinary life to the full centered in a relationship with God."[67]

This sophistry can only survive if one purposely ignores some very clear teaching in John that disproves McLaren's ideas. For example consider this section:

> *Truly, truly, I say to you, he who hears My word, and believes Him who sent Me, has eternal life, and does not come into judgment, but has passed out of death into life. For just as the Father has life in Himself, even so He gave to the Son also to have life in Himself; and will come forth; those who did the good deeds to a resurrection of life, those who committed the evil deeds to a resurrection of judgment.* (**John 5:24 – 29**)

67 McLaren, *Message,* 37.

Jesus is speaking of a future resurrection unto life or judgment, and not merely better living now with religion.

McLaren also redefines being born again according to John 3. After rejecting the idea that being born again is something that happens through some belief or experience he says this:

> No, Jesus is saying "Nicodemus, you're a Pharisee. You're a respected teacher yourself. But if you are coming to me hoping to experience the extraordinary life to the full I've been teaching about, you are going to have to go back to the very beginning. You're going to have to become like a baby all over again, to unlearn everything you are already so sure of, so you can be retaught."68

This is *not* what the passage says. It actually claims that rebirth or regeneration is a supernatural work of the Spirit of God, not a process of re-educating the sinner. Being born again is a work of God that cannot be explained by a natural process. If God did not do this work, it could not happen. McLaren explains it to be the opposite of what the passage teaches (i.e., a natural process of being retaught rather than a supernatural process of being regenerated).

Furthermore, McLaren's interpretation of John 3 ignores other Biblical passages about the new birth such as 1Peter 1:3 and 1Peter 1:23 as well as Titus 3:5-7, which teaches regeneration. None of these passages suggest a naturalistic idea of better living now through re-education or an interactive relationship with God.

The mission as understood by McLaren and other Emergent leaders also is described in terms similar to Liberation theology. Linking his idea of the kingdom to "the revolution of God," he sees the Emergent mission to be analogous to Dr. Martin Luther King Jr.'s fight against injustice and other social evils.[69] He sees the world as it is in terms of a "regime" in which some people oppress others by various means. He says, "This regime is unacceptable (an understatement I hope you recognize), and God is recruiting people to join a revolutionary movement of

68 Ibid. 38.
69 Ibid. 142.

change."[70] McLaren also uses other metaphors such as a party, a network, and a dance to illustrate what he thinks one is joining when helping God fulfill His dream of making the world into the kingdom without cataclysmic judgment.[71]

What is apparent in the Emergent, missional approach is that the words God inspired the Biblical authors to write, which authoritatively define the church's mission, are seen to be of little value. The mission is not derived from biblical exegesis, but from the thoughts and desires of the person who embarks on the mission. In short, the way Emergents read the church's mission means that the *reader* determines the meaning; the biblical authors do not. What they have determined is that one need not be a Christian to participate; salvation has nothing to do with avoiding future judgment or going to heaven; holistically saving planet earth is essential; changing society as a whole is essential; the church has not gotten the mission right in 2,000 years or even understood what it was; and that the Emerging Church is the best hope that, finally, God will be able to have His dreams fulfilled.

THE CHURCH'S MISSION AS DEFINED IN THE BIBLE

My research into the teachings and practices of the Emergent Church has uncovered an amazing irony. They routinely cast doubts on the perspicuity (clarity) of Scripture. (I will discuss this in a later chapter.) Supposedly the meaning of Scripture is cryptic—nearly impossible to understand—because of linguistic and cultural considerations and largely hidden. But reading the literature of Moltmann, Shults, McLaren, and others with similar theology is a most tedious and frustrating experience because *they* write in a cryptic, difficult manner, taking pains to be ambiguous, paradoxical, and vague. Compared with the pain of trying to understand them so I do not misrepresent what they believe, understanding the Bible is quite simple and straightforward.

To illustrate the point I will explain the Church's mission according to the terms found in Luke/Acts. We will see that it is rather clear. In Luke/Acts, Jesus gives His disciples their commission and explains how it will be accomplished. Acts then shows that it is actually accomplished in the very manner in which Jesus said it would be.

---

70 Ibid. 143.

71 Ibid. 146 - 148.

Here is Luke's description of the Church's mission: "*and He said to them, 'Thus it is written, that the Christ should suffer and rise again from the dead the third day; and that repentance for forgiveness of sins should be proclaimed in His name to all the nations, beginning from Jerusalem*'" (**Luke 24:46, 47**). Luke/Acts is a two-volume work written by one author (Luke) and shows itself to be a single work in two parts by internal consistencies and the introduction of themes in Luke that are not fully developed until Acts.[72] For example, at the end of Luke Jesus tells them to wait in Jerusalem to be clothed with power from on high and in Acts 2 that very thing happens.

This narrative unity can be seen in the commission to preach "repentance for forgiveness of sins." The theme of repentance for forgiveness of sins began much earlier in Luke. John the Baptist preached "repentance for the forgiveness of sins" (Luke 3:3). Jesus described His own mission as having come to "call sinners to repentance" (Luke 5:32). The angels in heaven are said to rejoice over "one sinner who repents." (Luke 15:7). Notoriously wicked cities would have repented had they seen the miracles Jesus performed (Luke 10:13). People who had perished at the hands of a tyrant and through a natural disaster serve as a warning about the fate of all who do not repent (Luke 13:1-5). It is impossible to miss the importance of preaching repentance. The two most important people in Luke (Jesus and John the Baptist, whose birth narratives are intertwined and spoken of in terms of divine visitation) preached repentance, and the disciples were commissioned to do the same.

Furthermore, Luke's two-volume narrative shows that the disciples faithfully carried out this commission. In doing so, Luke/Acts makes clear what is meant by repentance for the forgiveness of sins. Only the most contrived and confused reading of Luke/Acts could miss this emphasis. In Acts 1:8, Jesus told them how they would be used by the Holy Spirit: "*but you shall receive power when the Holy Spirit has come upon you; and you shall be My witnesses both in Jerusalem, and in all Judea and Samaria, and even to the remotest part of the earth.*" This is exactly what happened. In carrying out Jesus' commission, did they proceed along the lines Brian McLaren describes? That is, did they go out to make the world a better place, to tell industrialists to stop polluting, to cooperate with other religions in order to make the kingdom of God develop now through social

72 See Robert C. Tannehill, *The Narrative Unity of Luke—Acts – A Literary Interpretation* vol. 1 & 2 (Philadelphia: Fortress Press, 1986).

action, and teach other practices promoted by the Emerging Church? No! They obeyed Jesus and preached repentance.

The first example is prototypical as Peter (newly filled with the Spirit) preached to the crowd gathered for Pentecost. He indicted them for their sins (Acts 2:23, 36), and proclaimed Christ to have been crucified and raised on the third day, proving Himself to be the one to whom David pointed when he wrote that God's Holy One would not suffer decay (Acts 2:22-26). As Peter preached Christ and the resurrection some of his hearers were "pierced to the heart" (convicted by the Holy Spirit). They were now willing to respond in obedience as they asked, "What shall we do?" If McLaren's social gospel were the true mission of the church that would have been the time for Peter to tell it to those who were to become the first church, gathered together by the Holy Spirit. Had he done so, presumably Jesus' "secret message" would not have been lost for 2,000 years. But instead Peter said, "*Repent, and let each of you be baptized in the name of Jesus Christ for the forgiveness of your sins; and you shall receive the gift of the Holy Spirit*" (**Acts 2:38**).

Reading Luke/Acts as the two-volume work it is shows that Luke believed that Peter faithfully carried out Jesus' commission as cited in Luke 24:47. Here again is repentance for the forgiveness of sins. The early believers were baptized and they gathered around the apostles' teachings, breaking bread, and praying (Acts 2:41, 42). This is taught in Luke/Acts as a work of the Holy Spirit. This work of God did not unite world religions around good works to make life on planet earth a paradise now, but actually divided the church from early Judaism. This too was something Jesus predicted: "*Do you suppose that I came to grant peace on earth? I tell you, no, but rather division*" (**Luke 12:51**). Acts describes the division in stark terms as early Christians were persecuted by their former Jewish brethren.

To show that preaching repentance for the forgiveness of sins at Pentecost was not an isolated instance, the theme continues as the message of the gospel spreads along the geographical and cultural lines predicted in Acts 1:8. Peter again told his Jewish brethren to repent in Acts 3:19. When the gospel spread to God-fearing Gentiles (as recorded in Acts 10) and Peter explained to the other apostles that he had baptized Gentiles, they were finally convinced he was right to do so: "*And when they heard this, they quieted down, and glorified God, saying, 'Well then, God has granted to the Gentiles also the repentance that leads to life'*" (**Acts 11:18**). Being converted through the gospel was described in terms of having been granted repentance.

After Paul's conversion he becomes prominent in Acts, much like Peter was in the early part of the book. Did Paul understand Jesus' commission to preach repentance for the forgiveness of sins to apply only to the early disciples? No! Here is how Paul explained his own preaching in Ephesus: "*solemnly testifying to both Jews and Greeks of repentance toward God and faith in our Lord Jesus Christ*" (**Acts 20:21**). Acts even ends with the same theme that began with John the Baptist's preaching in Luke 3: "*but* [I Paul] *kept declaring both to those of Damascus first, and also at Jerusalem and then throughout all the region of Judea, and even to the Gentiles, that they should repent and turn to God, performing deeds appropriate to repentance* (**Acts 26:20**).

The church's mission is not cryptic in Luke/Acts, but is quite clear. How it was carried out by its early, Spirit-empowered leaders is normative. We are to preach repentance for the forgiveness of sins, including the proclamation of the person and work of Christ. People need to know that they are sinners facing judgment. They need to know who Christ is: His pre-existence, His virgin birth, His sinless life, His shed blood that averts God's wrath against our sins, His resurrection, and the threat that when He returns He will bring judgment, and that the wicked will be removed from the righteous and cast into hell (see Matthew 13:47 – 50).

We have a choice: We can follow the mission that Jesus gave the church as understood by the Apostles who gave us the New Testament, or we can become "missional" and find a more appealing mission by consulting other religions and our own "missional" community's sensibilities. The one is very clear and has been normative for 2,000 years. The other is confused, fuzzy, and unclear and was recently discovered by some innovative men. If we choose the latter we also are choosing to believe that Jesus' warnings about hell are false. That is a most dangerous choice to make.

Abstract Chapter 3

Undefining Christian Thinking

REJECTING THAT LANGUAGE CONVEYS UNDERSTANDABLE MEANING

Emergent leaders reject limitations or boundaries that language creates. According to their view, a dictionary, or even the concept of a dictionary, is foolish and impossible. In Emergent, every religious community creates its own "personal dictionary" and assigns meaning to words based on how they experience them. Because each community will experience and define words differently, it is absurd to believe that words themselves can convey truth or meaning to be understood by others. It is equally absurd to believe that an author's words can convey the thoughts that he intends the reader to understand. In Emergent, the reader is free to give whatever meaning he desires to the author's words. In short, language becomes a poor way to communicate truth because Emergent believes language is too uncertain to accomplish the task. For the Emergent, Christian thinking is not based on words, especially God's words. For them, spiritual experiences in a group setting are what lead to "Christian" thinking.

REJECTING THAT SCRIPTURES CONVEY UNDERSTANDABLE TRUTH

When "undefined language" is applied to the Bible (the words of God's authors) we can imagine how the Emergent Church's view of scripture differs from that of traditional Christianity. Since they consider words to be poor at conveying truth and meaning, Emergent leaders have embraced mysticism—where truth is *experienced* rather than understood. By making truth an experience, the Emergent have liberated themselves from the "constraining" interpretations of flawed and narrow-minded Christian theologians. If the words don't convey meaning but spiritual experiences do, language and thinking serve only as a springboard to mysticism.

"DECONSTRUCTION" DISCONNECTS LANGUAGE FROM UNDERSTANDING—CANNOT CONVEY TRUTH

The "deconstructed" view of the Bible and language in which meaning is removed (deconstructed) from words means that meaning is derived from freestyle spirituality. For Emergent, spiritual experiences are really the fastest and best path to the ultimate paradise that awaits us. Moreover, because deconstructed scriptures have no boundaries, we cannot doubt the spiritual experiences of others (whatever their faith). We must consider them to be as valid and meaningful as our own.

3

Undefining Christian Thinking

At my public debate with Doug Pagitt I brought up the term, propositional truth. A proposition is a truth claim that can be judged to be either true or false. Pagitt responded, "Why do you have to add adjectives to truth, isn't plain old truth good enough?" I was seeking to establish a definition of truth and how it is communicated–because adjectives help us clarify what we are talking about. He didn't like that clarification, apparently, and I have since found that the leaders of the Emergent Church are notorious for their unwillingness to believe that truth can be known in a way that is not culturally relative. The term "propositional" affirms that God speaks words that convey meaning and that Bible readers can understand God's meaning in a manner that binds them to its truth claims. That is why I use that term.

Though we will return to the subject of the Bible in chapter 5, where we will discuss how the Bible is understood and proclaimed, we also must deal with the Bible here because Christian thinking about matters such as the nature of truth and how one knows it is tied to how one understands God's self-revelation. Historically Christians have viewed the Bible as God's word in some sense. In their excellent work, *A General Introduction to the Bible*, Norman Geisler and William Nix provide a simple summary of three views of how the Bible is related to God's word: "The orthodox believe the Bible is God's Word;

liberals believe the Bible contains God's Word; the neo-orthodox hold that the Bible becomes God's Word."[73] By "orthodox" they do not mean "Greek Orthodox" but what they consider to be the true understanding that all Christians ought to hold. I hold the orthodox position.

Key evangelical leaders issued the *Chicago Statement on Scripture,* a 1978 series of articles that sought to preserve the evangelical doctrines of the authority and inerrancy of Scripture under attack by liberalism and neo-orthodoxy. Luminaries such as James Boice, John Gerstner, Francis Schaeffer, R. C. Sproul, and many others[74] produced this work. They defended the concept of verbal inspiration against those who claimed that self-revelation could not be propositional.[75] The arguments proposed by Emergent/postmodern theology are similar those used by existential, neo-orthodox theologians of the 20th century that Schaeffer and the others battled. This is shown by their rejection of propositional truth. Geisler and Nix include a glossary that includes this description of existentialism: "Religious existentialism holds, among other things, that revelation is not *propositional* but that it is *personal.* That is, it is not found in objective statements but only in a subjective and personal encounter with God."[76] Neo-orthodox theologians were strongly influenced by earlier existential philosophy.

Neo-orthodoxy is a sophisticated system of theology designed to "save" Christianity from liberalism. Scientific progress had made the claims of the Bible untenable in the minds of modern man, and liberalism responded by rejecting whatever parts of the Bible that did not fit their anti-supernatural bias, such as miracles. Their position was that the Bible *contains* the word of God, and they would determine which parts are still valid. The neo-orthodox position that the Bible *becomes* the word of God means that one has an existential, religious experience connected with Bible reading that is assumed to come from God.[77] Neo-orthodoxy believes that words are inadequate to convey binding revelation from God.

73 Norman L. Geisler and William E. Nix, *A General Introduction to the Bible* (Chicago: Moody, 1986) 171.

74 Ibid. 181.

75 Ibid. 185.

76 Ibid. 639.

77 Ibid. 188.

The Emergent approach to Scripture (which mimics neo-orthodoxy), with its attendant doubts about the ability to know propositional truth, has important ramifications for all Christian doctrine. It is not adequate to take Doug Pagitt's approach and demure from adding definitive adjectives to the term "truth." When the apostle Paul was brought before kings he testified about his encounter with the risen Lord. This caused Festus to question Paul's sanity:

> *And while Paul was saying this in his defense, Festus said in a loud voice, "Paul, you are out of your mind! Your great learning is driving you mad." But Paul said, "I am not out of my mind, most excellent Festus, but I utter words of sober truth. For the king knows about these matters, and I speak to him also with confidence, since I am persuaded that none of these things escape his notice; for this has not been done in a corner."* (**Acts 26:24-26**)

Paul's words were "sober truth" because they expressed truth about events that happened in history, before witnesses. The ideas expressed by his words could be judged to be true or false, so Paul spoke propositional truth. If what Paul was claiming existed only in his own mind, Festus would have been correct.

EMERGENT: "WHY CAN'T EVERYBODY BE RIGHT?"

Emergent writers decry any approach that declares some ideas to be true and others false. Propositions force people to decide what to believe. One Emergent writer, Dwight J. Friesen, explains his view: "The theological method of orthoparadoxy surrenders the right to be right for the sake of movement toward being reconciled one with the other, while simultaneously seeking to bring the fullness of convictions and beliefs to the other. Current theological methods that often stress agreement/disagreement, win/loss, good/bad, orthodoxy/heresy, and the like set people up for constant battles to convince and convert the other to their way of believing and being in the world."[78] Propositional

78 Dwight J. Friesen, "Orthoparadoxy - Emerging Hope for Embracing Difference," in *An Emergent Manifesto of Hope* Doug Pagitt and Tony Jones editors (Grand Rapids: Baker, 2007) 208.

truth claims do not fit into the Emergent "conversation" because they divide people. But the price of giving up such claims is to give up the very claims that the Biblical writers made.

Getting back to Paul's address before Festus and Agrippa, his words indeed got Agrippa's attention:

> *King Agrippa, do you believe the Prophets? I know that you do." And Agrippa replied to Paul, "In a short time you will persuade me to become a Christian." And Paul said, "I would to God, that whether in a short or long time, not only you, but also all who hear me this day, might become such as I am, except for these chains.* (**Acts 26:27-29**)

Paul believed that truth claims such as the bodily resurrection of Christ (Acts 26:23) were to be proclaimed even before kings who had the power over Paul's life. His was not a conversation with those who were just as likely to be right as Paul was, but a bold proclamation of the truth designed to convince others of the truth.

But the very practice of the New Testament apostles is what most Emergent leaders decry: claiming to be right about matters and anathematizing those who are in error. For example, Friesen says, "Here is my working maxim of a theology of orthoparadoxy: *the more irreconcilable various theological positions appear to be, the closer we are to experiencing truth.*"[79] Take careful note that he says "experiencing truth" (the neo-orthodox idea) not "knowing truth." Compare that to Paul's assessment of the Judaizers in Galatia: "*As we have said before, so I say again now, if any man is preaching to you a gospel contrary to that which you received, let him be accursed*" (**Galatians 1:9**).

Furthermore, Paul urged others to follow his example and charged elders with the duty of correcting false teaching: "*[The elder should be] holding fast the faithful word which is in accordance with the teaching, that he may be able both to exhort in sound doctrine and to refute those who contradict*" (**Titus 1:9**). Contrast Paul's instructions to Christian elders with the ideas of emergent writer Samir Selmanovic: "We have created a false tension between keeping our Christian identity intact and approaching the world in humility. Humility is to be our identity.

79 Ibid. emphasis in the original

When we open ourselves to be taught by 'the other,' we don't become less the followers of Christ but more so."[80] According to Paul we are to guard the flock against "the other" (i.e., religious beliefs that are not in accord with the faith once for all delivered to the saints) and in the Emergent view "the other" teaches us. Humility is not openness to false religions and false teachings; it is the realization that we are sinners who need a savior.

The real false tension is the one Emergent thinking creates between humility and confidence in the once-for-all revealed truth. Moses was called "humble" (**Numbers 12:3**) and to him was given the revelation of God's truth. Humble Moses told the Israelites not to listen to anyone who came in the name of a god they had not known—even if they produced signs (**Deuteronomy 13:1-4**). The idea that God's people would listen to false teachings as a sign of their humility is antithetical to what we are told in the Bible.

EMERGENT REJECTION OF TRUTH THAT CORRESPONDS TO REALITY

Emergent writers consistently diagnose conservative, evangelical Christianity as being captive to modernity/18th-century rationalism. What Emergent writers do not like is the quest for certainty about the truth that Christians have cherished. They claim that this desire for certainty is evidence that Enlightenment rationalism has found its way into the church. This, in turn, produces a naïve belief that we have arrived at the truth.

Stanley Grenz and John Franke continually use the term "demise" in relationship to any sort of approach to truth that considers itself foundational. For example, "In [their book's] previous chapter we indicated that one aspect of the emerging postmodern ethos that is especially crucial for the task of theology in the contemporary setting is the demise of the modernist approach to knowledge. The postmodern context is characterized by the widespread rejection of the foundationalism that characterized the Enlightenment epistemology."[81] Grenz and Franke believe that because certain philosophers have crossed Francis

---

80 Samir Selmanovic, "The Sweet Problem of Inclusiveness - Finding Our God in the Other," in *Manifesto of Hope,* 198.

81 Stanley Grenz and John R. Franke, *Beyond Foundationalism – Shaping Theology in a Postmodern Context* (Louisville: Westminster John Knox Press, 2001) 28.

Schaeffer's famous "line of despair"[82] and have given up on the possibility of knowing the truth concerning both God and His creation, Christians must now devise a theology that does not assume that certainty about the knowledge of the truth is a reasonable goal.

At the time Schaeffer was writing his books, the debate in evangelicalism was between evidentialists and presuppositionalists regarding the Christian defense of the truth. The evidentialists began by showing rational evidence that the Bible is true and therefore serves as our source of what Schaeffer called "true truth" (i.e., that which is from God, authoritative, and not to be doubted). Presuppositionalists rejected that approach. They started with the Bible (i.e., presupposing the Bible to be true) and from there built a system of theology and a Biblical worldview. But both approaches were foundationalist in the sense that they started with a foundation to build a system of truth. The Emerging Church rejects all foundationalism and views the previous evangelical debate between evidentialists and presuppositionalists as merely rearranging the deck chairs on the Titanic of modernity. (We shall return to this topic in chapter 7 where we discuss the Emergent theory about knowledge.)

Grenz and Franke explain: "The shaking of the philosophical foundations of the modern period means not only that the rules have changed but also that the time is ripe to ask new questions about how theology ought to be pursued. Indeed, the demise of foundationalism carries fundamental and far-reaching implications for theological method."[83] Having neither valid knowledge of history by which one could judge key Biblical claims like the bodily resurrection of Christ nor an inerrant, authoritative Bible from which one can gain an understanding of propositional truth, the postmodern theologian has to follow the path of current thinking in the philosophies of science and religion. Inevitably, that means some version of relativism.

These same postmodern theologies consider us hopelessly naïve—those of us who believe that the Bible is true in all it asserts and that one can glean from the Bible a systematic understanding of

82 Francis Schaeffer, *The God Who is There* (Downers Grove: Intervarsity Press, 1968). Schaeffer attributes this despair to rationalism that started with a closed system, examined the particulars, and sought to build a universal system of knowledge. His solution was not the rejection of rationality, but a return to the Reformation understanding of Scripture.

83 Grenz, *Beyond* 29.

God's revealed truth. For example, consider Grenz and Franke's critique of the great 19th-century theologian Charles Hodge's approach:

> Conservatives came to conclude that this invulnerable foundation lay in an error-free Bible, which they viewed as the storehouse for divine revelation. Hence, the great Princeton theologian, Charles Hodge, asserted that the Bible is "free from all error, whether of doctrine, fact, or precept." This inerrant foundation, in turn, could endow with epistemological certitude, at least in theory, the edifice the skilled theological craftsman constructed on it. . . . Conservatives such as Hodge grounded the error-free nature of scripture in its divinely inspired character.[84]

Grenz and Franke go on to mention the evidentialist approach, which looks to empirical evidence pointing to the truthfulness of the Bible and see it as foundationalist as well. If you are reading this and agree that Hodge's approach is perfectly sensible, you are (like I am) a naïve captive of the 18th-century Enlightenment in the eyes of the Emergent movement's leaders.

We assume things like the "correspondence theory of truth" and do not realize that this thinking also is a relic of a bygone era. What is the correspondence theory of truth? It is the idea that a statement is true if it corresponds to reality. For example, the statement "Jesus Christ was bodily raised from the grave" is only true if in fact a person named Jesus Christ actually lived and was, in fact, actually raised from the grave. If that seems obvious to you, once again you are a naïve captive of modernity. In their attack against foundationalism, Grenz and Franke state:

> The acceptance of the foundationalist approach, together with the presumed validity of metaphysical realism and the correspondence theory of truth, led conservative theologians to view the theological discipline as a science, understood in the modern

84 Ibid. 34.

> sense of the study of "the ordered phenomena which we recognize through the senses." Charles Hodge, for example, suggested that just as the natural scientist uncovers facts pertaining to the natural world, so the theologian brings to light the theological facts found in the Bible. Conservatives likewise assumed that the theological propositions they drew from the Bible stated universal—even eternal—facts . . ."[85]

But why shouldn't we consult the Bible to find the truth that God has revealed about Himself? These postmodern theologians obscure the fact that observing evidence allows us to establish facts that can be systematically understood as universal, eternal truth. This also was the practice of the Biblical writers themselves—long before the Enlightenment.

For example, consider Paul's argument in 1Corinthians concerning the validity of the gospel:

> *Now I make known to you, brethren, the gospel which I preached to you, which also you received, in which also you stand, by which also you are saved, if you hold fast the word which I preached to you, unless you believed in vain. For I delivered to you as of first importance what I also received, that Christ died for our sins according to the Scriptures, and that He was buried, and that He was raised on the third day according to the Scriptures, and that He appeared to Cephas, then to the twelve. After that He appeared to more than five hundred brethren at one time, most of whom remain until now, but some have fallen asleep; then He appeared to James, then to all the apostles; and last of all, as it were to one untimely born, He appeared to me also.* (**1Corinthians 15:1-8**)

Paul appealed both to Scripture and to eyewitness evidence in order to establish the eternal truth proclaimed through the gospel. Paul exhibits the same characteristics that are supposedly the product of

85 Ibid.

foundationalism. The Emergent thinkers who despise foundationalism can claim that the Biblical writers were as naïve as people like Charles Hodge, but they cannot deny that their writings exhibit the same tendency to think that truth can be gained through Scripture and observable evidence.

Emergent authors assume that some modern process robbed the church of something important that can be regained through a new version of reality. For example, Emergent author Tim Keel writes, "We took the world of the Spirit, of Scripture, of creation itself, and submitted it to Western, scientific rationalism."[86] In other words, we thought that the Bible meant what it said–that we can know that meaning–and that its meaning is accurately descriptive of the way things are. Keel suggests that we need mystics and "intuitive capacities" in order to access the new "version of reality" that characterizes the age we live in.[87] Notice, however, the relativism of his ideas. Reality does not come in "versions" but is, by definition, what actually exists. Philosophies come in versions, but reality remains unchanged. Keel laments, "In focusing so exclusively on our cognitive capacities, we have lost our imagination. We need mystics."[88]

This implies that using valid hermeneutics to understand the authoritative writings of the Bible does not provide the truth about the spiritual realities of the universe. In other words we cannot expect that God revealed Himself and the truth about His universe in propositions found in the Bible. Rather, we find these things directly through numinous, mystical experiences. Keel also suggests the right brain hemisphere can help us access what we have been missing: "They [seminaries] are training men and women for a world that no longer exists. We must begin to engage our brain's right hemisphere and make room for those for whom the right hemisphere is native landscape."[89]

The left brain/right brain dualism that Keel assumes is "true" shows the ultimate absurdity of postmodern relativism. How does he know that the brain hemisphere theory is true and that it needs to be

86 Tim Keel, "Leading From the Margins - The Role of Imagination in Our Changing Context," in *Manifesto of Hope* 229.

87 Ibid. 228, 229.

88 Ibid. 233.

89 Ibid. 232.

adopted into our theological approach? The brain hemisphere theories were developed by scientists studying people who had their two hemispheres separated for some reason such as surgery for epilepsy.[90] It gained interest among scientists because it was based on studies that relied on scientific methodology and observation. But the postmodern "right brain" popularizers question traditional scientific approaches to knowing the truth as being naïvely captive to modernity. So when something from "science" suits their fancy they adopt it and suggest we have to change which brain hemisphere we use in order to enhance our spirituality, while at the same time attacking the foundations that made modern science possible. The fact is that people who have not had surgery use both hemispheres of the brain and that the "pop" use of brain hemisphere theory is very questionable. John McCone has written to correct some of the myths of popularized versions of right brain/left brain theory.[91]

ESCAPE FROM REASON

When I first heard about the Emergent Church and read Brian McLaren's *A Generous Orthodoxy* in order to familiarize myself with its teachings, I immediately thought of Francis Schaeffer and three of his books: *The God Who is There; He is There and He is Not Silent;* and *Escape from Reason.*[92] Writing 40 years before McLaren, Schaeffer warned about the ideas that McLaren and other Emergents espouse.[93] In those works Schaeffer identified what he called "escape from reason" as a non-rational means of escaping the hopelessness of the results of rationalism.

Postmodern theology has much in common with the neo-orthodoxy that Schaeffer discussed. In fact an essay in *Emergent Manifiesto of Hope* praises Karl Barth and suggests McLaren is "not far from the theological project of Karl Barth."[94] Schaeffer discussed "...

90 http://www.singsurf.org/brain/rightbrain.php accessed April 23, 2008.

91 http://www.rense.com/general2/rb.htm accessed April 23, 2008.

92 These three books are still in publication as a one-volume trilogy. I recommend them because they show that Schaeffer was prophetic in his analysis of religious trends.

93 I wrote about this in CIC Issue 87, March/April 2005; http://cicministry.org/commentary/issue87.htm

94 Chris Erdman, "Digging Up The Past - Karl Barth [the Reformed Giant] as Friend to the Emerging Church," in *Manifesto of Hope* 237.

Karl Barth's system and the new theologies which have extended his system."[95] Here is Schaeffer's analysis:

> He held, and holds, the higher critical theories, so the Bible contains mistakes, but we are to believe it anyway. 'Religious truth' is separated from the historical truth of the Scriptures. Thus there is no place for reason and there is no point of verification. This constitutes the leap in religious terms.[96]

By "leap," Schaeffer means that everything having to do with religion or grace is put "upstairs" where it exists without the possibility of verification. Of course, once that happens, apologetics becomes impossible and all religious claims are equally valid. Why assume that Christian ideas of "truth" cannot learn something from Hindu ideas of "truth?" This is precisely what the Emergent Church movement suggests. As long as no verifiable, propositional truth about God is found through historical evidence for the resurrection of Christ or gleaned by logical implications and applications from inspired, inerrant Scriptures, there is no reason to think Christianity has any innate superiority to any other religion. All religious ideas exist only in a non-verifiable "upper storey" to use Schaeffer's famous term.

Schaeffer credits Kierkegaard with the existential "leap" to the "upstairs" where everything is disconnected from logic:

> What is particularly important to notice in this system is the constant appearance in one form or another of the Kierkegaardian emphasis on the necessity of the leap. Because the rational and logical are totally separated from the non-rational and the non-logical, the leap is total. Faith, whether expressed in secular or religious terms, becomes a leap without

95 Francis A. Schaeffer, *Escape from Reason* (Downers Grove, Intervarsity Press, 1968) 50.
96 Ibid. 51.

> any verification because is it totally separated from the logical and reasonable.[97]

As I read many books and essays from the Emergent movement my mind continually went back to Schaeffer's writings and this idea of the upper and lower "storeys"["storey" is Schaeffer's spelling and I will use that spelling when citing Schaeffer's concept]. People have developed more sophisticated systems of doubt than even Schaeffer had to deal with, but the problems are the same. An example is the idea of a socially constructed "reality." In the "real" world, people go about studies that assume the validity of observation, verification, repeatability, causality, non-contradiction, and other basic realities of how rational humans understand the world they live in; often they prosper in that world. The postmodern young person who joins the Emergent Church to escape the strictures of evangelical truth claims may very well undertake a course of study such as engineering where all the "foundational" approaches to knowledge are not only assumed to be true, but are successfully followed. Cars, roads, buildings, plumbing systems, and the like can be constructed because the foundational knowledge of the real world is valid. But then when it comes to religious knowledge, the same person takes the "leap" into the unknown and unknowable. Religion exists only in the non-rational "upstairs."

Schaeffer was right that "escape from reason" is actually "escape from God's authority." He also claimed that it was an escape from being human in the sense of bearing the image of God even in one's fallenness:

> Man, in the neo-orthodox theology, is less than biblical fallen man. The Reformation and the Scriptures say that man cannot do anything to save himself, but he can, with his reason, search the Scriptures which touch not only 'religious truth' but also history and the cosmos. He not only is able to search the Scriptures as the whole man, including his reason, but he has the responsibility to do so.[98]

97 Ibid.

98 Ibid.

Escape from reason in postmodernity is not caused by the same issues that caused the leap of faith in neo-orthodoxy. Those issues had to do with the fear that scientific knowledge had made the Christian faith untenable to modern man. Now all truth claims have become suspect as man supposes that reality is a state of consciousness.

The fear now is that people with bad motives have "constructed" a reality for us in order to control us. Many Emergent writers express their distaste for doctrinal boundaries such as those Schaeffer espoused, which were drawn by the Reformation. They are suspicious that knowledge of facts and doctrinal truth is really an attempt by the powers that be to create "structures of control" that are intended to keep others from expressing their alternative approaches to reality. So they imagine themselves in a socially constructed "reality" that can be deconstructed and reconstructed *ad infinitum,* or at least until they can find themselves in a preferable situation.

Before we leave Schaeffer's warnings and examine the idea of deconstruction, let us consider his warnings about the new mysticism:

> The significant thing is that rationalistic, humanistic man began by saying that Christianity was not rational enough. Now he has come around in a wide circle and ended as a mystic—though a mystic of a special kind. He is a mystic with nobody there. The old mystics always said that there was somebody there, but the new mystic says that that does not matter, because faith is the important thing. It is faith in faith, whether expressed in secular or religious terms.[99]

Schaeffer was absolutely correct when he warned that when we set out to disconnect our faith from both the Scriptures and the real world we will end up with mysticism devoid of content. His warnings went unheeded because we have ended up in a mystical morass with the Emergent Church leading the charge against Christianity with its verifiable, rational content that is binding upon all.

99 Ibid. 56.

Shaeffer's warnings are amazingly prophetic. Consider the following warnings from 1968:

> The evangelical Christian needs to be careful because some evangelicals have recently been asserting that what matters is not setting out to prove or disprove propositions; what matters is an encounter with Jesus. When a Christian has made such a statement he has, in analysed or unanalysed (sic) form, moved upstairs. If we think that we are escaping some of the pressures of the modern debate by playing down propositional Scripture and simply putting the word "Jesus" or "experience" upstairs, we must face this question: What difference is there between doing this and doing what the secular world has done in its semantic mysticism, or what the New Theology has done? . . . Certainly men in the next generation will tend to make it the same thing.[100]

They have made it the same thing and "they" are most fully seen in the Emergent Church movement. For example, consider the following: "And the artists, poets, prophets, contemplatives, and mystics among us have been witnessing to this [that facts are not adequate] from the margins for a long time. Artists and poets and others in our midst are in tune with the collective, intuitive, and spiritual. They have honored and then honed their sense and intuitive capacities . . . They are leading us somewhere."[101] They are indeed. They are leading us away from reason, and in so doing, away from God's authoritative words binding us to anything. They are leading us to a religion that erases boundaries and exists as an undefined experience.

Schaeffer further warned:

> If what is placed upstairs is separated from rationality, if the Scriptures are not discussed as open to verification where they touch the cosmos and history,

100 Ibid. 77.

101 Keel, "*Leading*" in *Manifesto of Hope*, 228, 229.

> why should one then accept the evangelical upstairs any more than the upstairs of the modern radical theology? On what basis is the choice to be made? Why should it not just as well be an encounter under the name Vishnu?[102]

The answer is that in our generation it has become just that—Emergent leaders call it "an openness to the other." Any mystical practice is useful when there are no definitions and Scripture does not bind anyone to propositional truth. Thinking and religion are de-linked from the real world through mystical practices, and thereby have no logical boundaries. One can create a religious world of one's own pleasing. Evangelicals failed to listen to Schaeffer's warnings, and we have found ourselves right where he said we would be:

> Increasingly over the last few years the word 'Jesus,' separated from the content of the Scriptures, has become the enemy of the Jesus of history, the Jesus who died and rose and who is coming again and is the eternal Son of God. So let us take care. If evangelical Christians begin to slip into the dichotomy, to separate an encounter with Jesus from the content of the Scriptures (including the discussable and the verifiable), we shall, without intending to, be throwing ourselves and the next generation into the millstream of the modern system.[103]

We have done just that; but now it goes by the name "postmodern."

SOCIALLY CONSTRUCTED REALITY AND DESCONSTRUCTION

In the book, *A is for Abductive*, Sweet, McLaren and Haselmayer explain in an entry under "deconstruction" that deconstruction is an important concept for the Emergent Church [104] but that it is "difficult

---

102 Schaeffer, *Escape*, 77.

103 Ibid. 79

104 Leonard Sweet, Brian McLaren, and Jerry Haselmayer, *A is for Abductive – The Language of the Emerging Church* (Grand Rapids: Zondervan, 2003) 87.

for outsiders to understand." A suggestion found at the end of the entry says: "Readers will probably learn more about deconstruction through a single thoughtful viewing of the movies *The Matrix* and *The Truman Show* than through re-reading this entry a hundred times."[105] Let us consider *The Truman Show*.

In that film, Jim Carrey plays a man who lives in what he thinks is a real "world" but in reality is a set of a real-life soap opera. He was born on the set. All his life he was made to believe that it was all there was of the real world. Each of the others in his life were actors who conspired to keep him thinking his world was real for the sake of the audience. His idyllic world eventually begins to yield clues that it is not so real, such as a spotlight falling into his yard. As he gets more and more suspicious that there is more to the world than the island he is on, and for some reason can never leave, he decides to escape. At the end of the film, Carrey's character steps through the artificial boundary of the set and into the real world. But is this "new world" actually the "real" one, in the postmodern sense?

Deconstruction assumes that, like the producer in *The Truman Show*, authorities have conspired to make us believe that the limited and constricted version of our "world" is all there is. This conspiracy exists for the profit of the colonizers who keep people unknowingly trapped in a world they never chose to be in. (McLaren uses the colonial period as a metaphor for the ailments of Western Christianity.[106]) Emergent authors regularly complain that they felt taken advantage of by evangelicalism, which too narrowly defined their "reality."

Deconstruction is often applied to literary texts. In the aforementioned entry in *A is for Abductive*, Sweet, McLaren and Haselmayer state, "[Deconstruction is] An approach to interpretation of literary texts (and film and other media) that begins by questioning many of the assumptions of traditional interpretation. For example, traditional interpretation assumes that the author's conscious intent is a (or the) primary concern in interpreting a text."[107] Indeed, authorial intent is the key to understanding written communication and is the governing principle in hermeneutics—but not for the postmodern

105 Ibid. 90.

106 Brian McLaren, "Church Emerging - Or Why I Still Use the Word Postmodern but with Mixed Feelings," in *Emergent Manifesto*, 149.

107 Sweet, *Abductive,* 87.

reader. The new assumption is that writers have hidden motives that must be uncovered in order to determine the real meaning of their words. In the minds of some in the Emergent Church those motives are "command and control" and the spread of white, euro-centric, male dominated Christianity over others. Hints of such motives are ferreted out in written material.

Literary deconstruction has serious ramifications for the interpretation of Scripture. For example, Sweet and his co-authors state, "Traditional interpretation generally assumes a logical structure and deep coherence of texts; in other words, the author meant to say something sensible and did so in a coherent way. Deconstruction looks for points of inherent tension, contradiction, and incoherence."[108] This means that the hermeneutic where authorial intent determines meaning and that the use of sound grammatical/historical analysis of the text reveals that meaning is no longer valid. In my opinion, deconstruction gives the reader rather than the author control over the meaning.

One can see the perverse affects of this postmodern approach to texts in many Bible studies that are far too common nowadays. A portion of Scripture is read and the question, "What does that mean to *you*?" is posed. So rather than seeking the singular meaning of the Biblical author, the group shares various feelings about how they respond to the text. The authority of Scripture becomes a meaningless concept because the Bible no longer binds anyone to one valid meaning.

Deconstruction also doubts that language corresponds to reality: "Moreover, traditional interpretation has worked within the larger modern worldview in which language is believed to correspond quite strongly and neatly with reality. In this view, our words correspond to things in reality outside of our minds in a simple, commonsense way. . . . Deconstruction sees this confidence as naïve."[109] Schaeffer warned about a Jesus separated from the verifiable content of Scripture as the enemy of the Jesus of the Bible. The Emergent use of deconstruction makes naïve at best the Biblical Jesus (described by the Biblical authors) as descriptive of the real Jesus in verifiable history. Thus McLaren discusses seven Jesuses experienced in various

108 Ibid.

109 Ibid. 87, 88.

churches rather than attempting to articulate a Biblical doctrine of Christ.[110]

It is further suggested that we have to give up the goal of finding the true meaning of the Bible if we want to reach the postmodern person: "For example, every time preachers or authors seek to interpret Scripture, they make it clear by their assumptions and method which interpretive community they belong to. By driving for 'the one true interpretation,' for example, they disenfranchise postmodern readers for whom deconstruction is as much the mother tongue as traditional interpretation is for modern people."[111] That means that if a culture chooses to believe that truth cannot be authoritatively conveyed via human language, the preacher of the gospel must accept their judgment on the matter and preach to them authoritatively neither Christ nor the gospel.

This, too, creates the "upper and lower storey" scenario that Schaeffer decried. What if one tried to take the principles of deconstruction into a court of law? Suppose a person was on trial for breaking and entering and armed robbery. The criminal broke down a locked door, entered a private home, held up the homeowner at gunpoint, and stole his property. Upon being brought to trial, the man turns out to be a postmodern robber. The prosecuting attorney reads the charges against him and includes the homeowner's eyewitness testimony and the physical evidence. The robber responds, "You are naïvely holding to the correspondence theory of truth." As the trial proceeds, the state laws against breaking and entering as well as armed robbery are read. The robber responds, "You naïvely assume that you know the meaning of the words of the interpretive community that wrote those laws, and furthermore naïvely assume that you can read those words and make them correspond to something in your version of reality which I may not share."

The absurdity of trying to apply the principle of deconstruction to a criminal proceeding shows that it can only exist in some "upper storey" realm disconnected from real life. The truth is that throughout human history people have been validly communicating–

110 Brian D. McLaren, *a Generous Orthodoxy* (El Cajon, CA: Youth Specialties, 2004; published by Zondervan) 43 - 67.

111 Sweet, *Abductive,* 89.

and cross-culturally at that. Human commerce would come to a halt if legal documents and binding contracts did not function according to "the correspondence theory of truth" as the Emergent writers call it. If our written and spoken words were unable to rightly describe things in the real world that are validly meaningful to us and to those who read or hear us, we would find ourselves back in the situation in which the builders of the Tower of Babel found themselves when God confused their languages. Everything would stop immediately. But in reality, human communication has never been more powerful than it is today.

Another absurdity is that the writers of Emergent books are using the norms of language to communicate their ideas to people who do not share their "interpretive community" (people like me, for example). They expect us to understand them. But if they were so sure that understanding written texts is basically futile, why do they bother to write books? They depend on the human ability to communicate validly about the world we live in—the ability God gave us when He created us in His image—and then spend their time denigrating that ability.

A friend of mine was required to take a hermeneutics class that used a postmodern writer's text. This author's basic hermeneutic held that it was impossible to determine the Biblical authors' meaning because of all the supposed problems, such as "interpretive communities" and so on. The bottom line for all such approaches is "the reader determines the meaning." So my friend, frustrated with having to read that particular book, had to write a report about it. So he wrote the following: "What this book means to me is: what the Bible says is true, meaning is determined by the authors of the Bible, and meaning can be understood by modern readers." The professor was not happy, but what could he say? If the reader determines the meaning (and my friend *was* the reader), how could his version of the meaning be wrong? If he was told his understanding of the book's meaning was wrong, then the professor's entire theory is proven to be wrong.

We will end up with absurdities no matter how we try to apply deconstruction and the postmodern understanding of communication. But even the fact that we see these absurdities is supposedly caused not by the theories themselves, but by our connection to modernity: "While desconstuction feels to moderns like chaos and nihilism, it feels to postmoderns like honesty and liberation. While moderns feel deconstruction yields readings that are unclear, slippery, unserious, and unscientific, postmoderns feel that deconstructive readings are meaningful, interesting, playful, rich, honest, rewarding and inclusive."[112]

I am quite certain they would not feel that way if they had to be consistent and apply the same approach to all of life. Would they want the doctor to deconstruct the medical journals to his own suiting before making a diagnosis of their illness? Would they want the airline pilot to deconstruct the instructions from air traffic control and find his own suitable way to land? If they were defrauded through a broken contract, would they want the legal experts to deconstruct the contract in order to suit the fancy of the person who defrauded them? Postmoderns only find deconstruction useful when they apply it to such things as religion, philosophy, and morality. I can state that because I see young people having been fed this type of thinking in college successfully occupying jobs and professions that require valid real-world communication. They have simply put the rest of life in an "upper storey" where reality need not apply.

DESPAIR OR HOPE?

The thinking espoused by the Emergent Church should produce despair, not hope. How could it be hopeful to exist in the film *The Matrix* and be unable to know conclusively that one was "there?" Even if we escaped this "matrix" we could never know if the next one were any closer to reality. That is the ultimate situation of hopelessness with respect to knowing the truth.

Remember, Emergents believe God to be at work in the process of history and drawing everything toward a better reality. If this were true, each paradigm shift would get closer to the future reality where the kingdom of God would be realized. This false belief gives an *illusion* of hope as an utterly hopeless system of thinking is embraced: "*Always learning and never able to come to the knowledge of the truth*" (**2Timothy 3:7**). We will examine how this approach undefines Christian teachings in the next chapter.

112 Ibid.

Abstract Chapter 4

UNDEFINING CHRISTIAN THEOLOGY

EMBRACING REAL CONTRADICTIONS—THE IRRATIONAL

Removing words' meaning (deconstruction) leads to the capacity to embrace contradictory positions simultaneously because the words then become fluid—definitions morph as we "experience" rather than hold to meaning. Emergent considers it normal and even beneficial to hold beliefs that are incompatible with each other. Believing both sides of a contradiction is considered beneficial because Emergent believes that the meanings will evolve (synthesize) into a new and better belief. Emergent teachers' rejection of solid definitions results in theology and beliefs that reject logic and boundaries. Emergent refuses to be bound by rational thought because truth and meaning are *experienced* rather than *known*.

TYPES OF KNOWLEDGE—GENERAL REVELATION AND SPECIFIC REVELATION

God has given humanity five senses and a rational mind in order to discover and learn about His physical creation and to learn using logic. Discovering facts about the creation with reason and our five senses is called "general revelation." General revelation is what our economy, industry, and scientific achievements are based upon. It is part of "cause and effect." While humanity understands that through general revelation and His creation that there is a God, His plan of salvation (which means being reconciled to our Creator) is not found in general revelation. God's plan of salvation and reconciliation is found *only* in scripture (specific revelation), spoken to humanity through human mediators (i.e., through prophets and the man Jesus Christ). Scripture reveals a God who issues commands that He expects to be understood and obeyed. He is a God who hates sin and who will judge all sinners. This same God, because He loves these sinners, sent His own Son to take their punishment and offer them reconciliation. This "revelation of good news" is not found via general revelation, through science, or by observing nature. It is only found in Scripture, the words of God conveying this meaning to the reader.

SPIRITUAL TRUTH KNOWN THROUGH MYSTICAL EXPERIENCES—NOT SCRIPTURE

Because Emergent deconstructs the meaning of God's words and looks to spiritual experiences for truth and meaning, the resulting "spirituality by experience" is no different than pagans' pursuit of God. Spiritual experiences and spirituality itself have been important to mankind since recorded history began. The problem is that this pursuit of mystical experiences always leads to idolatry and damnation, and not to the God revealed in scripture. Only God's revelation via scripture provides His plan of reconciliation: "There is no other name under heaven given among men by which we must be saved."(Acts 4:12) Emergent, by embracing freestyle spirituality and "meaning through experience," is simply old-fashioned paganism using modern terms, language, and practice. We are not to seek meaning and truth through spiritual experiences but through words—the words of God Himself—written down by men who saw Him, touched Him, and heard Him with their physical ears. (1 John 4:1)

4

Undefining Christian Theology

During the Pagitt debate I showed a PowerPoint slide that contained the following quotation from his book, *Preaching Re-Imagined*:

> So what is a church to hold to if it isn't a classic statement of faith? I suggest holding to all the church has held to throughout its history. If a belief is in harmony with historical Christianity, then it should be seen as a valid position. This means people will often hold contradictory positions, but that's a good thing.[113]

I took issue with this on the grounds that historical Christianity has been filled with various heresies and that contradictions are meaningless. I gave examples such as the conflict between the Biblical position of the deity of Christ and Arianism, which claimed Jesus Christ was a created being. Both views were held in church history. At one time Arius had much of the church following his ideas. But both Arius and Athanasius, who led the fight against him, could not be right. If Christ was created He lacked the essential nature of deity, which in-

113 Doug Pagitt, *Preaching Re-imagined – The Role of the Sermon in Communities of Faith* (Grand Rapids: Zondervan, 2005) 133.

cludes eternal, non-contingent existence. The contradictory positions could not coexist as "orthodox."

Interestingly, when it came to the rebuttal portion of the debate, Pagitt asked to have the PowerPoint slide about holding contradictory positions returned to the screen. He reaffirmed what he wrote as well as the validity of contradictions. I claimed that a contradiction was analogous to a square circle—one can say the words but conceptually it is meaningless. To state that Jesus Christ existed from all eternity, as God and with God (John 1:1), and that He was a created being who, at some point in the past did not exist, is to make an absurd and meaningless statement. To claim to believe both sides of a logical contradiction is to fail to communicate anything meaningful. That is precisely the mode of "communication" favored by the leaders of the Emergent Church—and it is distressing that many support it.

Brian McLaren exhibits the same tendency to favor contradictions. The subtitle of *a Generous Orthodoxy* illustrates it: "Why I am a missional + evangelical + post/protestant + liberal/conservative + mystical/poetic + biblical + charismatic/contemplative + fundamentalist/Calvinist + Anabaptist/Anglican + Methodist + catholic + green + incarnational + depressed-yet-hopeful + emergent + unfinished Christian."[114] Can valid Christian theology be built on the foundation of contradictions? The answer is no because contradictions communicate nothing whatsoever, much less truth.

The Emergent Church loves being playful and provocative at the expense of definitions. That is why many local Emergent congregations reject statements of faith. Pagitt writes: "For many pastors, statements of faith set the boundaries for the sermon. The problem is that statements of faith usually serve to keep people away from the church more than they draw them in."[115] But the rejection of boundaries is in fact a rejection of Christian theology at its very core. To go back to the Arian controversy in Church history, Christian statements of faith affirm the deity of Christ. This affirmation is indeed a boundary. It does set boundaries for one's sermons because one cannot affirm the deity of Christ then preach the Arian slogan, "There

---

114 Brian McLaren, *a Generous Orthodoxy* (Youth Specialties: El Cajon, CA, 2004; published by Zondervan).

115 Pagitt, *Preaching*, 132.

was a time when He was not." This is true of the other articles of the Christian faith also.

What about the claim that such boundaries "keep people away?" Let us assume that an Arian (Jehovah's Witnesses hold to the same heresy today) considered attending a church. If, in fact, the church does believe in the deity of Christ, would not a visiting Jehovah's Witness expect that the church leaders would state their belief? If Jehovah's Witnesses refuse to attend any church that believes in the deity of Christ, it is their rebellion against the truth of the Bible that keeps them away, not the fact that the church is willing to confess Christian beliefs publicly. The Emergent approach is to take the public posture of embracing "the other" so they can make everyone comfortable in their churches.

LOGIC AND BOUNDARIES

The Emergent embracing of postmodern thought as theology's foundation (as evidenced in the postmodern theology of Grenz and Franke, mentioned earlier) leads to a rejection of the use of logic to define categories. This came up several times in the Pagitt debate. In my opening presentation I purposely used logic to show that God uses words to draw boundaries, something I knew Pagitt and other Emergents would deny. The logic went as follows, using a series of disjunctive syllogisms (either/or arguments):

Either: Boundaries for religious activities to approach God exist.
Or: No boundaries for religious activities to approach God exist, and we can come to Him freestyle.

That syllogism forces one to decide if "all paths lead to God" or some paths do not. Then:

Either: God determines the terms and means of salvation and sanctification.
Or: We are free to come to God for salvation and sanctification on our own terms and by creating pathways to God from our own imagination.

That syllogism, assuming that the correct answer to the first is that there are boundaries, forces one to decide whether the terms of how one comes to God are determined by God or man. The next one forces a decision about whether such boundaries have been revealed by God:

Either: God defines pathways to approach Him in the Bible—interpreted literally according to the intent of the author communicating objective propositional truth for our understanding.
Or: Men can create their own pathways to God through imagination—freestyle boundaries which are self-referential, mystical, contradictory and/or irrational.

The latter option is the option that the Emergent Church has chosen.

The next piece of logic was a hypothetical syllogism[116] (an If/Then statement):

If: There are no Divinely revealed boundaries to religious activities and religious innovators show us the way to God.
Then: A sincere community of Mormons, Hindus, Muslims practicing spirituality and demonstrating ethical benevolent behavior would be just as near to God as a Christian community embracing the gospel.

The "if" in the hypothetical statement was Pagitt's position—he said so in his books. The "then" leads to an unacceptable outcome for Bible-believing Christians, but apparently not for the Emergent Church.

Pastor Pagitt's response? He accused me of employing "binary reductionism," and further stated that he didn't like reducing life to either/or statements. That means there are options other than the two sides presented. It is true that the only way to logically defeat a disjunctive syllogism is to prove there is a valid third option; if such is found, the syllogism is shown to be false. I commend him for his

116 Norman L. Geisler and Ronald M. Brooks, *Come Let Us Reason – An Introduction to Logical Thinking* (Grand Rapids: Baker, 1990) contains description of the types of syllogisms and their usage in logic. Ironically, my logic professor in seminary was LeRon Shults, whose writings express the type of postmodern theology favored by the Emerging Church.

tactic. By labeling my logic "reductionism" Pagitt implied that there was such an option.

For the sake of being complete and comprehensive, let us examine the statements one by one to see if any reasonable third options exist: When it comes to approaching God, either boundaries exist or they do not. That statement is valid. Any statement claiming that something either exists or does not exist is true by nature—there is no possible third option. The second syllogism assumes that universalism is false and that there are boundaries. This paints the Emergent theologians into a corner because they do not want to reveal before an audience of Christians that they think there are no boundaries. From my research, I conclude that the key leaders of this movement are universalists but prefer to hide that fact.

But since the only choice that avoids universalism is that some boundaries exist, the next step is to decide who defines them—God or man. What is the third option that would defeat my syllogism? We can narrow the possibilities because only an intelligent, communicative being can define a boundary for religious activity. Other than God and man the other options are spirit beings, such as demons and angels. It would be absurd to state that demons would be a valid third option for determining the boundaries of religious activities to come to God since, by definition, they are evil and work to keep us from God. So the only possible third option is the holy angels. Since holy angels are blameless and do God's bidding, even if they were used as intermediaries to reveal boundaries the resultant boundaries would still be God's. So the syllogism stands and is not reductionist as Pagitt claimed.

The next syllogism has to do with plenary, verbal revelation and pushes the issue a step further to determine how the boundaries are discovered. Has God determined the boundaries by revealing objective, propositional truth through the Bible, or is man free to experiment using various religious activities if he is to find his way to God? We have not yet decided on God or man; we simply have narrowed it to the two options. But now we must decide. If God exists and is transcendent, spiritual, and would not be known in a personal way unless He decided to reveal Himself, either He has or has not revealed Himself to man in a way that man could comprehend and be held accountable to. Postmodern theologians cannot escape these realities no matter how badly they wish to. If God has spoken, then we are accountable to what He has revealed. If what God has said can be known in a non-relativistic way and He has revealed boundaries to religious practices including how we come to God and how we should live, then those boundaries are fixed. Otherwise humans may create their own religions and hope that if there is a personal God in the universe, He will accept whatever religious practices they invent with their own imaginations.

This is not binary reductionism, but rather a description of the most important issue in Christian theology: has God spoken? If He has, can we understand? If we can understand, are we accountable? I say yes in wholehearted agreement with a chorus of Christian theologians through the centuries. But the debate revealed that Pagitt and other Emergent leaders like him are not willing to join that chorus.

Furthermore, one cannot deny that the Bible makes this claim: "*God, after He spoke long ago to the fathers in the prophets in many portions and in many ways, in these last days has spoken to us in His Son, whom He appointed heir of all things, through whom also He made the world*" (**Hebrews 1:1, 2**). The Bible also makes many claims that are obviously exclusive, some of which I asserted in the debate. For example, in Acts 17 Paul said that God has furnished "proof" to all men through the resurrection of Christ, and therefore all are accountable to repent (Acts 17:30, 31). One would assume that any Christian would agree on these matters because they are the most foundational of all the Christian beliefs. God has spoken through His ordained prophets and has spoken most profoundly through His Son.

The issue is whether or not we will accept what God has said and make it the bedrock of any theological discussion. Pagitt rejected even these basic ideas as "reductionist." So I asked him later whether or not Mormons would have a valid Emergent church if they wanted one. He refused to answer on the grounds that the question was hypothetical.

Later we discussed the validity of the most important foundation of logic, the law of non-contradiction: *A is not non-A at the same time and in the same relationship*. I said that if this is not valid, it is impossible to define categories. Pagitt refused to acknowledge the validity of non-contradiction and claimed that it does not work on a subatomic level. This is a claim that New Agers also use in order to justify their mysticism.[117] My rejoinder was that when studying physical chemistry at Iowa State University I had to write equations in order to describe activities at a subatomic level. If non-contradiction does not work, one cannot describe the process with an equation. All that can really be said is that there is more to reality than what we are able to describe adequately. But without non-contradiction, nothing can be described. Descriptions delineate things from one another. We arrived at neither agreement nor compromise.

HAS GOD SPOKEN?

The issues of Emergent theology and Emergent thinking described in the previous chapter are very closely related. In order to escape from God's boundaries, one must first escape from the validity of verbal communication that accurately and validly describes categories. This issue can be illustrated from the Bible's account of the Garden of Eden: "*Now the serpent was more crafty than any beast of the field which the Lord God had made. And he said to the woman, 'Indeed, has God said, "You shall not eat from any tree of the garden"?'*" (**Genesis 3:1**). Is God's verbal communication valid? God had indeed spoken: "*The Lord God commanded the man, saying, 'From any tree of the garden you may eat freely; but from the tree of the knowledge of good and evil you shall not eat, for in the day that you eat from it you will surely die*'" (**Genesis 2:16, 17**). If non-contradiction is false, then A and non-A can be the same at the same time and in the same relationship. Through verbal communication the forbidden tree could not be distinguished from the non-forbidden trees. Furthermore, eating and dying could not be proven to be different than eating and not dying. The attack on non-contradiction is an attack on verbally described boundaries.[118]

Furthermore, the Emergent Church calls its approach to theology a conversation. What they mean by that is that one never assumes that some ideas are true, others are false, and that one can

---

117 There is a chart here http://www.xenos.org/CLASSES/papers/quantum.htm that examines mystics' use of quantum physics and contains rebuttals. (accessed May, 2008).

118 See Bob DeWaay, The Validity of the Law of Non-contradiction for Religious Epistemology; http://cicministry.org/scholarly/sch004.htm

know oneself to have true ideas that are incompatible with false ideas held by others. The process always is a conversation that might lead to some sort of enlightenment. So applying it to Eve, she cannot know that the idea God gave her (that she would die if she ate) was true, and she should be open to "the other" who may just as well possess the truth. So she entered a conversation: "*The woman said to the serpent, "From the fruit of the trees of the garden we may eat; but from the fruit of the tree which is in the middle of the garden, God has said, 'You shall not eat from it or touch it, or you will die'*" (**Genesis 3:2, 3**). She did not quite accurately describe what God said, but she did get the "die" part right. The Serpent continues the conversation: "*The serpent said to the woman, 'You surely will not die! For God knows that in the day you eat from it your eyes will be opened, and you will be like God, knowing good and evil'*" (**Genesis 3:4, 5**). The truth and meaning of God's verbal communication was questioned and categories were erased. The boundary drawn by God's inerrant words was then transgressed when Eve and then Adam rebelled. The conversation led to "enlightenment"–the knowledge of good and evil which the Serpent claimed was a desirable outcome.

A conversation gave birth to all the sorrows and evil in the world through the Fall. (We will return to this "conversation" in the next chapter in order to analyze the way postmoderns use the Bible.) Theology built on a foundation of a conversation in which coming to the knowledge of the truth is not even an expected outcome will not lead to paradise (unless, of course, the Hegelian synthesis is true and the paradoxes and contradictions are simply precursory to better options that will arise as God pulls history to Himself savingly on a "tractor beam of redemption," as Tony Jones says). Then all paths lead to God, and it really does not matter what theology one holds. Perhaps a square circle is not meaningless like I claim it to be, but is a concept to keep in mind until a new reality emerges.

THE EMERGENT REJECTION OF SYSTEMATIC THEOLOGY

When discussing theology as evangelicals have traditionally understood it, Emergent writers and postmodern theologians use disparaging terminology such as "freeze-dried, shrink-wrapped, or fossilized."[119] For example, LeRon Shults writes, "At the other extreme,

119 McLaren, *Generous*, 286, uses the freeze-dried and shrink-wrapped analogy.

[from those who would dissolve the Christian faith through engagement with "the other"] some are tempted to respond *paleo*-constructively, resisting engagement with culture in order to stay behind with the "same" fossilized formulations of Christian intuitions that have been unearthed from modern (or premodern) discourse. The danger here is the petrification of Christian faith."[120] Shults is speaking of systematic theology in obvious derogatory terms.

His characterizations are unfair and misleading. Theological statements derived from careful Bible study then written in carefully crafted language go back at least to the Nicene Creed. What era of history they stem from (modern, pre-modern, or postmodern) is not the issue; what matters is whether or not they accurately describe Biblical truths in such a way subsequent generations can defend them if necessary. But previously it was a given that if theologians of subsequent generations wanted to question the content of a previous statement of theology, whether it was the Nicene Creed, the Definition of Chalcedon, the Westminster Confession, Charles Hodge's systematic theology, or any other systematized statement on a range of Biblical subjects, they had to do so on the grounds that any such statement did not accurately reflect the true teachings of the Bible on the topic. Throughout the ages the best of these statements, such as Chalcedon, have stood the test of scrutiny. Theologies written in the so called "modern" period (which is blamed by Emergent writers for most of the perceived "ills" of the church) were not written with the idea that they were the final statement on all things theological. They were written because, as history rolls on, philosophers and theologians ask different questions. There always has been a need to address those questions in a systematic way based on the timeless and changeless truths of Scripture.

Furthermore, whatever doctrines have been articulated in the past are challenged by theologians who disagree. When that happens the challenges ought not to be left unrequited. For example, when Hodge wrote his systematic theology he addressed Deistical Rationalism, the moral government theory of the atonement, and so forth. When Millard Erickson wrote his systematic theology in the late 20th century (the one I was required to study in seminary), he addressed

120 F. LeRon Shults, *Reforming The Doctrine of God* (Grand Rapids: Eerdmans, 2005) 3.

challenges such as neo-orthodoxy, process theology, and other matters not even presented as options in Hodge's day. But both Erickson and Hodge came from the perspective that, most importantly, one had to determine whether currently proposed theologies were Biblical. Postmodern theologians would place both Erickson and Hodge in the category of "modern" and see them to be held captive to the Enlightenment. For example, Pagitt claims that sermons in which a pastor proclaims and applies Biblical truth to the congregation (something he calls "speaching") are the "creation of Enlightenment Christianity."[121] Never mind that Paul told Timothy to preach in such a manner 1,700 years before the enlightenment (2Timothy 4:1-4).

My point in making this in rebuttal to Shults and other Emergent or postmodern theologians is that it is false to claim that the works of past theologians were "fossilized." Theologians of the past showed a willingness to deal with new issues as they arose in church history. What *is* "fossilized" in the approach is the Bible itself. Previous systematic theologies, whatever qualities and merits they may have possessed, were written from the perspective that the Bible contains the once-for-all revealed truth that can be applied to the questions that arise in any era of history. Theological formulations are adjusted to address whatever currently poses a threat to the "faith once for all delivered to the saints." The Bible *never* changes; it is the *terms* that theological formulations use in order to apply Biblical truth to current issues that change. So rather than complaining that theology is fossilized, Shults, Pagitt, McLaren, and the others should aim to be more accurate and complain that the Bible is "freeze-dried and shrink-wrapped," if by that they mean that the faith "once for all delivered to the saints" as Jude says.

What is different in postmodern theology is that the Bible no longer is seen as the only infallible source for settling the truth of a theological issue. Pagitt writes:

> The contemporary church makes two mistakes regarding the function and relationship of the Bible. One is to think of her [Pagitt calls the Bible "she" and "her"] as a stagnant telling of all the desires of

121 Pagitt, *Preaching*, 60.

> God. The other is to think of her as something from which we extract truth, whether in the form of moral teaching or propositional statements.[122]

We do not claim that all the "desires of God" are found in the Bible, but only those which God has chosen to reveal. Furthermore, if we cannot "extract truth" from the Bible, which informs us theologically about the important issues such as creation, salvation, sanctification, morals, atonement, and future judgment, then the Emergent Church is correct in stating that systematic theology is a fool's mission. But where do we go if Holy Spirit-inspired words cannot reveal God's mind on a matter?

The answer (for Emergent Church writers and writers of post-modern theology) is to go to general revelation, linguistics, church tradition, human culture, philosophical speculation, to construct one's own theology. So having disparaged the idea that the Bible can be understood, applied and can serve as God's ordained means for understanding spiritual truth, they go to a multitude of sources so complex and convoluted that the resultant theologies are incomprehensible to most. This is particularly true of Shults, while Grenz and Franke are not much better. Shults is so obscure and opaque that even Tony Jones, who admires this type of theology, said that Shults is too abstract for many people to access. Yet before Shults left Bethel Seminary for Norway, he was teaching required theology classes at that Baptist seminary.

WHEN THEOLOGY IS NO LONGER DERIVED FROM THE BIBLE

My colleague and friend Ryan Habbena had the unhappy experience of studying theology under Shults. Habbena reported that anytime a student wished to discuss a traditional Christian doctrine that one would typically expect to study in a theology class, Shults would dismiss that as "Enlightenment rationalism" and imply that the students were simply too ignorant to understand his postmodern theology.

The problem with Shults and others of the postmodern mindset is that they do not distinguish between special revelation

122 Ibid. 44.

and general revelation. They do this by lowering the Bible to the level of general revelation and then sifting through it to find nuggets that can be further modified by philosophy and science. Shults shows this tendency when he cites 1Corinthians 6:17 about the Christian being "one spirit" with God and then goes to general revelation to interpret it.[123] The following extended Shults citation shows how this process works in his postmodern theology:

> Let me state the thesis even more strongly: the longing for unity with the divine that one finds in various myths of world cultures, in the structures of human self-consciousness, and in philosophical reflection on metaphysics, is fulfilled in and through the spiritual regeneration of those who become "one spirit" with the Lord. The anthropological analysis points toward a fulfillment in the theological domain, while the theological doctrine discloses the creaturely integrity of anthropological self-understanding. I will suggest a specific way of defending the scriptural language about the relation of the Holy Spirit to human spirit as both coherent and experientially adequate. The goal is not to "prove" a Christian doctrine based on neutral foundations, along the lines of early modern natural theology, but simply to present the explanatory power of the Christian claims about Jesus Christ as the transformer of human identity. My strategy is to engage in the interdisciplinary dialogue with philosophy and cultural anthropology, which attempt within their own disciplinary guidelines to describe the nature and structure of the human grasping after union with the divine.[124]

This dense and confusing paragraph tells us that the Bible has no special explanatory power about spiritual truth and that *anything* found in nature or human history can be valid sources from which to build

123 F. LeRon Shults, *Reforming Theological Anthropology* (Grand Rapids: Eerdmans, 2003) 77.
124 Ibid. 78-79.

a theology. Shults' approach lacks any exegetical work that would discover Paul's meaning in 1Corinthians 6:17. Was Paul concerned with how humans understand "union with the divine" in some metaphysical sense? If we consult the Biblical passage we find that Paul's concern was that because Christians are "joined" to the Lord spiritually, they are a temple of the Holy Spirit and should therefore never be "joined" to harlots (1Corinthians 6:16-20). In postmodern theology, adherents rarely consult the intended meaning of the Biblical author. Such consultation would be to "prove" a doctrine based on what Shults calls "early modern natural theology" (i.e., the "naïve" idea that one could find timeless truth of God by searching the Scriptures).

The result of that postmodern approach is a theology that does not take special revelation (what God has spoken once for all) to be foundational. After all, they call their approach "post-foundational." This means that Biblical ideas do not express the mind of God in a manner that is timelessly binding on all Christians throughout the ages (in whichever culture they may exist). Phrases and concepts such as regeneration are pulled from the pages of Scripture and analyzed through the lens of contemporary anthropological theory—without even giving reference to what the Biblical authors meant by the terminology. Shults goes on to use complex mathematical set theory and logical formulations akin to differential calculus to propose an understanding of regeneration. Here is the result:

> A theoretical mathematician would say that the agent is "hypostatized in the domain" (a phrase that is at least suggestive for potential dialogue with Christology). Because we are talking about stories, these "domains" denote modes of agential existence. If we believe that God created the proportional structures of the universe and the patterns reflected in the intelligibility of human consciousness (embodied first in the mathematical intuitions of small children), then it should not come as a shock that the dynamics of regeneration produced by the Holy Spirit would fulfill the longing of our created spirits, which are

> embedded in the proportionality of spatiotemporal existence.[125]

Reading Shults may suggest to people that they are not smart enough to understand Christian theology. The book I am citing was required reading for his seminary students, some of whom longed to actually learn traditional Christian doctrine.[126] Instead they had the arduous task of trying to understand everything from quantum physics to evolutionary biology–*before* learning Christian theology.

Interestingly, when Shults finally gets to discussing Biblical passages, he does so to refute the doctrine of original sin, claiming that it came from Augustine's theories and not from Paul's teachings in Romans 5.[127] The sources for the postmodern theology of the Emergent Church are so dense that even well-trained students of theology have great difficulty understanding them. I found the process to be rather painful as I completed the research for this book. Reading the likes of Moltmann, Shults, and, to a lesser degree, Grenz, strained my abilities to concentrate and correctly understand their claims. I have been reading Christian theology for more than 35 years and have theological degrees–but what about people with no such training? It is no wonder that Christians have problems understanding the Emergent Church. I do not think I am being unfair when I say that beneath all the sophisticated verbiage is a not-so-veiled agenda of denying the most basic doctrines of the Bible–the substitutionary atonement, original sin, and so on.

What we need to understand about their approach to theology is this: Their theology is no longer derived through the exegesis of Biblical passages. When they reject systematic theology they reject the idea that God has spoken authoritatively through Scripture and that what God has spoken through the Scriptures is consistent and reveals truths that can be understood systematically–like the doctrine of original sin. When they left proper exegesis, they created a theological free-for-all.

---

125 Ibid. 81.

126 A friend of mine, Eric Douma, was one such student. I accompanied Eric to discuss his concerns with the provost of the seminary.

127 Shults, *Anthropology,* 189 - 210.

A THEOLOGY GROUNDED IN SILENCE?

McLaren, in a chapter describing why he is "mystical/poetic," suggests that mysticism and silence are valid, while rebuking systematic theologies for their "arrogance:"

> There long have been Christian traditions recognizing the profound importance of mysticism and poetry, and the corresponding limitations of rationality and prose, including the *via negativa*—the negative way—and the *hesychastic* tradition, which discovers God in silence. Both traditions remind us of the limitations of language when talking about God, a subject so great that no words can do it justice.[128]

McLaren's attempt to escape reason is a not-so-thinly veiled attempt to escape the authority of Scripture. If human language is inadequate for speaking about God, is it also inadequate for God to speak to us about Himself? That is the issue, and McLaren obscures it. If we had to speak about God with no specific revelation from Him about Himself, then surely our speech about God would be entirely inadequate. But God has spoken! How dare McLaren suggest that mysticism and silence are more adequate ways to know theological truth than with rationality and words! God has spoken, and His words and our ability to rationally understand and apply them is the only way to know about God and come to Him on His terms. Those who "enter the silence" have no way of knowing whether they have encountered the true God who created the world or a demonic impostor.

It is bad enough that rationality and language are disparaged, thus rendering the Bible irrelevant and inaccessible, but McLaren also sees fit to attack Christian theology traditionally articulated (i.e., derived from the Bible and applied to the important questions):

> This rebuke [the one cited above that promotes "the silence"] to arrogant intellectualizing is especially apt for modern Christians, who do not build cathedrals of stone and glass as in the Middle ages, but rather

128 Brian D. McLaren, *Generous*, 151.

> conceptual cathedrals of proposition and argument. These conceptual cathedrals–known popularly as systematic theologies–were cherished by modern minds. . .[129]

According to this thinking, a systematic theology discussing matters such as the communicable and incommunicable attributes of God is arrogant intellectualizing, but entering the silence is a valid way to know about God. That is why I entitled this chapter "Undefining Christian Theology." The whole idea of theology is to study about and speak about God (Greek *theos*-God and *logos*-word combined to form the word). Silence can do neither. Theology, by its postmodern definition, has become meaningless. Words cannot speak about God, so we cannot speak about God, and presumably God cannot speak about Himself. It makes no sense.

POSTMODERN THEOLOGY AS NEO-PAGANISM

Postmodern theology does not start with God and His self revelation but, according to Shults, starts with the individual's experience: "Rather than beginning with the idea of the all-powerful will of a single divine subject, and then *later* trying to make sense of Scripture and religious experience, I am suggesting that we instead attempt to illuminate the issue of divine agency from within the categories that structure our lived experience in community, reaching out in a transversal dialogue that is always open to being reformed."[130] The tragic thing about such thinking is that it mimics the methodology that has always characterized paganism.

Pagans throughout history have had no special, verbal revelation from God that came to them via infallible spokespersons for God, such as Moses. Pagans had to begin with their experiences in community and their environment and from it, construct a theology. They had nothing else on which to build. The result was polytheism, child sacrifice, abusive priesthoods, and irrational stories about gods and goddesses with morals worse than most humans.

---

129 Ibid.

130 Shults, *Doctrine of God*, 253.

So why would we think that to abandon the doctrine of the clarity of Scripture for relativistic theories about socially constructed reality, and to seek our theology from general revelation rather than special revelation (i.e., from nature rather than the Bible) will lead us toward the truth and a better world? The answer is found in the eschatology (as we argued in chapter 1) adopted by the key leaders of the Emergent Church and theologians such as Grenz and Shults: God is the future drawing everything into Himself. Shults calls this "eschatological ontology"[131] and cites Moltmann and Pannenberg as key contributors to this view. Here is Pannenberg as cited by Shults: "God is the future of the finite from which it again receives its existence as a whole as that which has been."[132] Supposedly all finite things and beings are on a trajectory toward God in a way imagined by panentheistic theologians who see the world sort of as the negative polarity of God that has evil in it but must be drawn back into God so that all will be good.[133]

The speculations of these postmodern theologians are more sophisticated and civilized than the speculations of ancient pagans, but they are predicated on the same premise—we can only know God by observation, speculation, and experience. To them, special revelation no longer has a unique place in informing us about God and the world He created. The Bible tells us that God created the world out of nothing; that is how it begins. It then tells us man is created in His image, elevating our status to rational beings above the rest of the creation. Then it tells us that God spoke rationally with words to Adam and Eve. It then tells us of God as lawgiver and the Serpent as tempter. It tells us of the Fall and a plan of redemption through the seed of the woman. But casting aside the only means by which we can know the truth, the Emergent Church and the postmodern theologians they learn from have sadly taken the role of the Serpent themselves as they question, "Has God said."

They use Biblical terms like "Holy Spirit," and they cite Bible verses massaged in such ways that fit their worldview. If asked how they know they are on a trajectory (a favorite word in their theologi-

131 Ontology is the study of being.

132 Shults, *Doctrine of God,* 191.

133 There are many versions, and not all would describe their view this way. The polarity analogy is from process theology.

cal writings) toward a better understanding of God and the truth, they often answer, "The Holy Spirit is working in the Christian community to bring us closer to God." But the *huge* flaw in this is that absent the clear, authoritative words spoken by God's appointed, infallible speakers (the Biblical writers), there is no way to "test the spirits" (1John 4:1-5). Moltmann continually speaks of the experiences of the Israelites and interprets them as "hope." Shults speaks similarly: "Already in the Hebrew Bible, the righteous Israelite's experience of trembling delight in the divine reign point to the irreducibly social dimension of the human experience of good and evil. The Christian community is called to participate in the redemptive fellowship of divine goodness, which moves (in)to the world as the infinite power of love, giving itself for the other."[134] The emphasis is not on God's words spoken through Moses that explain His covenant relationship and the terms thereof, but on experiences as interpreted by a community.

This process cannot make certain that the community experiences interpreted as loving and good are the product of the work of the Holy Spirit. They may just as well be a counterfeit from Satan that deludes a particular community into thinking they do not need the blood atonement to be right with God. Their "rightness" is self-referential in that it is not validated by anything objective and outside of themselves. Being in a community doing good deeds does not prove that God is at work. The confession of the person and work of Christ who "came in the flesh" is the objective standard. If the gospel is not preached according to the terms revealed in the Bible, the "good" that is deemed from "the Holy Spirit" may be a delusion. Mother Theresa was well known for doing good deeds, but in the end, it has become known, was found to have lived a life of despair–she did not confess the gospel as her only hope. Just doing "good" does not provide assurance that one is right with God and that the person will escape future judgment.

McLaren, after several pages of undermining the idea of a systematic theology that explains propositional truth about God, reveals the consequence of moving from revealed truth to the mystic/poetic and conversational, community approach: "We must, therefore, never underestimate our power to be wrong when talking about God, when thinking about God, when imagining God–whether in prose or in

134 Shults, *Doctrine of God,* 250.

poetry."[135] Precisely! That is why we must *start* with what God has spoken to us about Himself, not with ourselves and our conversations.

This brings us back to boundaries and the Pagitt debate. Can we come to God any way we see fit, or has God revealed the way to Himself? That is the basic question. Is the answer found in specific revelation (God has spoken) or in general revelation (the creation and our own religious experiences)? The "freeze-dried" Christian theology rejected by the Emergent Church holds that if God had spoken authoritatively on a topic through the Biblical writers, the truth about that topic could be ascertained and described systematically. The postmodern approach rejects that in favor of speculation and conversation as one interprets his own experiences.

The former theological method of systematic theology also required that all pertinent topics were covered and that the writer of the theology defend his view from Scripture. It was unthinkable for a systematic theology to have no entry under future judgment, atonement, and so on. But the theological method of the Emergent Church allows them to skip any topic they do not like. They do so without seeing a need to defend their view Biblically when they reject doctrines such as the blood atonement and future judgment. Silence is an acceptable "answer" for them.

Having undefined theology, they are free to speculate and declare themselves immune from criticism. After all, they are merely having a conversation and are not making any absolute truth claims. The fact is they *do* have a theology, and it is not at all compatible with the most important Biblical truths. The implication of their theology is that all paths lead to God in a saving way. If this turns out to be false, many eternal lives will be lost when the conversation finally comes to an end.

---

135 McLaren, *Generous,* 153.

Abstract Chapter 5

Undefining the Bible and Preaching

GOD'S WORDS PURSUED IN SPIRITUAL EXPERIENCES IN A COMMUNITY SETTING

The message of the Emergent church rejects using our minds, logic, and reason to understand the words God spoke to humanity because, they say, scripture does not convey a fixed meaning determined by the Biblical, Holy Spirit-inspired authors. The Emergent believe God's commands and His directives concerning salvation and the coming judgment are impossible to know based on His words because their meaning simply is not found there. They seek meaning and revelation of God through spiritual *experiences* pursued together, in community with others. The words of the scriptures may be read and debated, but the experiences of all individuals in the group determine what the passage means at that particular time. God's commands evolve as people "experience" meaning together; therefore God's commands are no longer universally binding. In the future the same passage or command may evolve to present a different meaning as collective experiences of the congregation provide new meaning.

In scripture, God commands us to study, understand, and believe His words and to obey His commands. He, with His finger, wrote real words in the Hebrew language in stone. He holds us accountable to understand the meaning of His words. Through the death of His Son on the cross and through the gift of the Holy Spirit, God has provided us with a new nature–one that embraces His commands joyfully. Thus, for the Christian, the means to grow in sanctification and holiness is to better understand and believe God's words. We come together on Sunday morning as a church to listen to God's word spoken and applied to our lives. As good readers, we attempt to understand what meaning the Author of the Bible wished to convey to us.

SHARED SPIRITUAL EXPERIENCES THE BASIS FOR FELLOWSHIP

This is very different in the Emergent Church. Spiritual experiences become the true source of meaning for individuals and the congregation. Words, even the words of God, do not convey the meaning we need. Thus, the Emergent Church leaders embrace methods and practices that encourage these experiences because this is where they believe they find the growth that hastens the appearance of the coming paradise. The more this concept is embraced, the less important the scriptures become and the more important the mystical spiritual experiences become.

5

Undefining the Bible and Preaching

One of the most profound changes away from what most Christians have believed throughout the centuries is the Emergent and postmodern practice regarding how God's word is understood and proclaimed. In the classical view, God's word expresses His revealed truth, and Christian preachers are obliged to accurately and authoritatively preach it. Now, all that is being changed based on the conclusion that the meaning of the Holy Spirit-inspired Biblical authors cannot be accurately known across various cultures. One implication of this doubt is that if we proclaim a certain meaning of the Bible to be binding on all, we are guilty of a sinful attempt to manipulate and control others.

The Emergent Church doesn't want to allow the possibility that we can know Biblical truth, so they call their endeavor a "conversation." And all opinions are valid in this conversation. It is ironic that, according to the Bible, all of the evils in the world are the result of a conversation between the Serpent and Eve. I introduced this idea in chapter 4, and we will explore it here at greater length.

The situation began with God speaking to Adam and Eve clearly and authoritatively: "*And the Lord God commanded the man, saying, "From any tree of the garden you may eat freely; but from the tree of the knowledge of good and evil you shall not eat, for in the day that you eat from it you shall surely die*" (**Genesis 2:16, 17**). God's words were not difficult to interpret and apply. The first humans were free to partake of God's bounty as they saw fit—with one exception: God's revealed law forbade them to eat from just one particular tree, and it specified the penalty if they broke it.

The narrative continues with the Serpent starting a conversation with Eve: "*Now the serpent was more crafty than any beast of the field which the Lord God had made. And he said to the woman, 'Indeed, has God said, 'You shall not eat from any tree of the garden'?*" (**Genesis 3:1**). Hebrew scholars point out that the Serpent's words mean, "did God *really* say?"[136] Furthermore the Serpent changed the command to make it sound overly strict and prohibitive ("not eat from *any* tree"), whereas God actually permitted them to eat from every tree but one. Gordon Wenham calls this, "a total travesty of God's original generous permission."[137] So the conversation begins by questioning and altering God's clear statement.

The woman's part of the conversation also involved a movement away from God's word. Whereas Genesis 2 refers to Him as "the Lord God," which invokes the covenant name, the Serpent, and then in her response, the woman, refer to Him merely as "God."[138] The woman also changed God's word in her statement: "God has said, 'you shall not eat from it or touch it, lest you die'" (**Genesis 3:3b**). Kenneth Matthews gives a good summary of how Eve misrepresented God's Word:

> The woman's first mistake was her willingness to talk with the serpent and to respond to the creature's cynicism by rehearsing God's prohibition (2:17). However, she compounded her mistake by misrepresenting God's command as the serpent had

136 Mathews, K. A. (2001, c1995). *Vol. 1A*: *Genesis 1-11:26* (electronic ed.). Logos Library System; The New American Commentary (235). Nashville: Broadman & Holman Publishers. This is expressed in the ESV translation: "Now the serpent was more crafty than any of the wild animals the Lord God had made. He said to the woman, "Did God really say, 'You must not eat from any tree in the garden'?"

137 Gordon J. Wenham, "Genesis 1 - 15," in *Word Biblical Commentary*, (Dallas: Word, 1987) 73.

138 Matthews, 235.

> done, although definitely without the malicious intent of the snake. The serpent had succeeded in drawing the woman's attention to another possible interpretation of God's command. It would seem that the serpent had heard it all differently! Now the woman changes the tenor of the original command. First, she omits those elements in the command, "any" and "freely," which placed the prohibition in a context of liberality. At this point she still is thinking collectively with her husband, from whom, as the narrator implies, she received the command: "*we* may eat" (v. 2). Second, Eve identifies the tree according to its location rather than its significance; and third, she refers to "God" as the serpent had done, rather than "the LORD" (v. 3). Fourth, she also adds the phrase "you must not touch it" (v. 3), which may make the prohibition more stringent. Yet to her credit the fear of touching the fruit may have been out of deference for God's command. For Israel "touch" was associated with prohibition and death or with consecration to God. Finally, she failed to capture the urgency of certain death, "You will *[surely]* die" (v. 3).[139]

So by engaging in a conversation with a being that was not committed to God's inerrant word, Eve was seduced by "another possible interpretation" as Matthews calls it. This led to listening to the Serpent's outright contradiction of God's word when he said, "*You surely shall not die*" (**Genesis 3:4b**). Then these progenitors of the human race rebelled and plunged all of their descendants into sin and death.

Emergent and postmodern theologians accuse those of us who believe that the Bible speaks clearly, inerrantly, and authoritatively of being "naïve." They prefer a conversation that begins with the premise that our knowledge of the Bible has been filtered through so many cultural grids that our theological beliefs cannot have been

---

139 Ibid.

gained directly through Biblical interpretation. Stanley Grenz and John R. Franke make that very claim:

> At the same time, however, the unidirectional pattern that moves from biblical studies to theology suffers from several debilitating difficulties. Not the least of these is its naivete about the purported objectivity of exegesis, a naivete that is indicative of the Enlightenment or modernist hermeneutical assumptions from which it operates.[140]

Theirs is a fancy way of stating, "Has God said?" The idea that what God has said must be known and believed in order to avoid deception, sin, and all the attendant consequences did not arise from the Enlightenment—it is found in Genesis! God expects what He said to be known, understood and believed. The result is true "theology" (belief about God and His will). Eve's theology ran amok because her conversation with Satan was predicated on the idea that what God said was questionable.

I do not sensationalize when I state that Emergent/postmodern theology has taken on the Serpent's role of questioning the objectivity of God's word. For example, an Emergent writer rejects "dogmatic" statements: "The problem with orthodoxy or authoritative dogmatic claims is that they are conversation stoppers."[141] But "The day that you eat from it you will surely die" was *intended* to be an authoritative dogmatic claim, and had it been a "conversation stopper" world history would not abound with evil, sin and death.

"THE HOLY SPIRIT TOLD US"

Grenz and Franke attempt to rescue a meaningful Bible by employing the old neo-orthodox approach that claims the Holy Spirit is at work in the *reading* of the Bible (at least in a group) in order to supply meaning. They claim that the meaning of the Holy Spirit-inspired au-

140 Stanley Grenz and John R. Franke, *Beyond Foundationalism – Shaping Theology in a Postmodern Context* (Louisville: Westminster John Knox Press, 2001) 84.

141 Dwight J. Friesen, "Orthoparadoxy – Emerging Hope for Embracing Difference," in *An Emergent Manifesto of Hope* Doug Pagitt and Tony Jones editors (Grand Rapids: Baker, 2007) 211.

thors cannot be known by any valid hermeneutic; instead meaning is found through the reading process. Do not be fooled. Sophisticated as it may sound, it still questions "has God said." In their version, God has not yet spoken until a community reads.

> We read knowing the Spirit speaks through scripture, appropriating the text so as to create our communal world through it. While the world the Spirit fashions is specific to our situation and hence is not merely a transplanting of the world of the text into the present, the Spirit-constructed world we inhabit is nevertheless shaped by the world disclosed in the text. Our world is to be the contemporary embodiment of the paradigmatic narrative of scripture constructed through the interpretive framework that emerges from the Bible as a whole.[142]

This describes their "dialogical approach"—necessitated by "the non-objectivity of all biblical exegesis"[143]—a fancy way of saying, "the reader determines the meaning of the text." In this case, since we supposedly cannot know objectively the Spirit-inspired authors' meaning, the Holy Spirit instead inspires a community of readers who then find their own, unique meaning. This dialogical process is precisely the one adopted by the Emergent Church and is the ecclesiastical result of postmodern theology. Let us consider some of the problems.

Going back to our Genesis example, the statement "the day that you eat of it you will surely die," was God's own; God, who uttered the words, determined the meaning. The text does not create the meaning, it transmits meaning to readers. The first two "readers" to interact with the text were Eve and the Serpent. They were the first "interpretive community" to carry on a "dialogical approach." Immediately the ideas conveyed by God's words began to morph into other forms. At that point, how would one determine whether or not the Holy Spirit was guiding the process? Do we have some *a priori* way to judge whether the dialogical process is creating a "Spirit-constructed

142 Grenz and Franke, 85.

143 Ibid.

world" as opposed to a "Satan-constructed world"? If so what is it? If we say, "we can judge this based on the fact that they were departing from what God said," we would be correct, but that assumes there is such a thing as "objectivity of exegesis," which has already been denied by Emergent and postmodern theologians.

That leaves us with a question: How do we know we are proceeding in the right direction? The answer: We need to determine what a "Spirit-constructed" world looks like. But since the Spirit-inspired meaning of the text has been ruled out on the grounds that it is inaccessible and the objective approach has been nullified, we are left with only various subjective ones. The Emergent approach, as seen in Brian McLaren's *The Secret Message of Jesus*, is to define the kingdom of God in terms of making the world a better place, and then to judge anything that appears to promote that agenda to be the work of the Holy Spirit. McLaren says, "A new force, a new spirit is in the world–not a demonic spirit, but the Holy Spirit. Just as sick, destructive spirits can take possession of groups, this new Spirit is entering people and forming them into a healthy, creative, and new kind of community or society–the kingdom of God."[144] His understanding of the "secret message" is the social gospel, where if "good" things are happening, the Spirit is at work.

But as has always been the case, this pragmatic test for truth fails. We need to know what is true before taking certain actions or joining a certain "interpretive community in dialogue." This, too, can be illustrated by the Serpent and Eve. The Serpent assured Eve that a better world would be the result of accepting his understanding of theology. He explained the benefits as not dying, becoming like God, and having enhanced knowledge (good and evil). By the time Eve discovered that the outcome of her dialogue was horrible evil and the curse it was already too late. If we don't first know the truth, we cannot (contra McLaren) be sure that our actions are a work of the Holy Spirit bringing in the kingdom of God. (We will discuss the Emergent idea of the kingdom more fully in chapter 8.)

For example, what if McLaren and the other Emergent leaders who agree with him are wrong? What if rather than the kingdom of

---

144 Brian McLaren, *The Secret Message of Jesus – Uncovering the Truth That Could Change Everything* (W Publishing Group: Nashville, 2006) 66.

God gradually manifesting itself through social action leading toward a paradise on earth, the coming kingdom is actually a *threat* that will bring irrevocable judgment to all who have not repented and believed the gospel? What if the point of the church in history is to preach the gospel so that those converted become citizens of the kingdom and that the coming kingdom happens when Christ returns in judgment? In that case the following scenario would play out: "*While they are saying, 'Peace and safety' then destruction will come upon them suddenly like birth pangs upon a woman with child; and they shall not escape*" (**1Thessalonians 5:3**). By then it will be too late then to find out that the social gospel is false. Like Eve in her dialogue with the Serpent, people must first decide what to believe, because competing truth claims can result in dire and irrevocable outcomes—especially if they believe the wrong message. I claim that judgment is coming, so we must have our sins washed away by the blood of Christ so that when that day comes we shall be saved rather than damned. McLaren claims that the kingdom is coming gradually through social action and we need not be concerned about such matters as God's wrath and the need for the blood atonement. We cannot both be right. If we wait for history to prove which argument prevails, it will be too late—at least "too late" if judgment is coming.

This means we need to make a decision now: Which is the true work of the Holy Spirit? The "interpretive community in dialogue" that is working toward a utopian social outcome through cooperation with "interpretive communities" of other religions, or the church that finds its beliefs from objective exegesis of Scripture? When the outcome comes to pass, it will be too late to decide. Adam and Eve were cast out of paradise and not given the opportunity to rethink their theology. When the kingdom of God comes, and some find themselves in the wrong conversation about a wrong message promoting a wrong agenda, there will be no opportunity to turn back:

> *Again, the kingdom of heaven is like a dragnet cast into the sea, and gathering fish of every kind; and when it was filled, they drew it up on the beach; and they sat down, and gathered the good fish into containers, but the bad they threw away. So it will be at the end of the age; the angels shall come forth,*

> *and take out the wicked from among the righteous, and will cast them into the furnace of fire; there shall be weeping and gnashing of teeth.* (**Matthew 13:47-50**)

If there is a future judgment as Jesus described it, we need to know (objectively) the terms of the judgment before it happens. It will not be enough to be in a dialogue with an uncertain outcome.

When it comes to matters such as eternal life, subjective judgments are entirely inadequate. For example, suppose a person considers Hinduism as a better "interpretive community" because he or she admires the social actions of some Hindu guru. Hinduism assures us that through reincarnation the soul continues to have many opportunities to live in different bodies until it is perfected and reunited with the Divine. Christianity teaches that after living once on the earth there is judgment (Hebrews 9:27). What if a person lived in a Hindu interpretive community, worked for the same social ends as the Emergent Church, and trusted that there will be many more lives to get things right–and then died and found out the Christian idea was true? Obviously it would be too late to avoid eternal punishment. Religious truth claims have eternal consequences; they must be judged by objective means before the consequences of believing them come to pass. On that ground alone, the postmodern "conversation" utterly fails and must be rejected.

THE BIBLE'S CLAIMS ABOUT ITSELF

The frustrating thing about discussing or debating theology with Emergent and postmodern theologians is their failure to acknowledge many obvious claims that the Bible makes about itself. For example, let us consider this one:

God, after He spoke long ago to the fathers in the prophets in many portions and in many ways, in these last days has spoken to us in His Son, whom He appointed heir of all things, through whom also He made the world. (**Hebrews 1:1, 2**)

The Biblical claim is that God has spoken and has done so through the Scriptures. The Emergent/postmodern attack is not leveled directly against the Bible, but rather against the possibility of knowing its meaning. God has spoken, but (according to them) no one is sure what He said.

Consider McLaren's ideas about this as He discusses Martin Luther's dispute with Rome: "Martin Luther's famous individualistic statement, uttered before the Catholic authorities with whom he disagreed, expresses the shift perfectly: 'Here I stand.'"[145] McLaren calls this, "[T]he first statement uttered in the modern world."[146] The great problem in the minds of postmodern scholars is the "humanness" of Biblical interpreters—the "I" who does the interpreting. The following extended quotation from McLaren illustrates the reason the Bible cannot function authoritatively for postmodern thinkers:

> How do "I" know the Bible is always right? And if "I" am sophisticated enough to realize that I know nothing of the Bible without my own involvement via interpretation, I'll also ask how I know which school, method, or technique of biblical interpretation is right. What makes a "good" interpretation good? And if an appeal is made to a written standard (book, doctrinal statement, etc.) or to common sense or to "scholarly principles of interpretation," the same pesky "I" who liberated us from the authority of the church will ask, "Who sets the standard? Whose common sense? Which scholars and why? Don't all these appeals to authorities and principles outside the Bible actually undermine the claim of ultimate biblical authority? Aren't they just the new pope?[147]

According to this thinking Luther took us from the Pope to the Bible, but when he believed that a person (like Luther) could know what the Bible means and take a stand based on that meaning, he made a new "pope" out of Biblical interpretation.

145 Brian McLaren, *a Generous Orthodoxy* (El Cajon, CA: Youth Specialties, 2004; published by Zondervan) 132, 133.

146 Ibid. 133.

147 Ibid. 133.

The Bible says, "God has spoken" but the Emergent approach says, "yes but we cannot know *what* He spoke." But did the Biblical writers share this doubt about knowing the meaning of God's inspired words? Consider what the author of Hebrews says in the book's second chapter:

> *For this reason we must pay much closer attention to what we have heard, lest we drift away from it. For if the word spoken through angels proved unalterable, and every transgression and disobedience received a just recompense, how shall we escape if we neglect so great a salvation? After it was at the first spoken through the Lord, it was confirmed to us by those who heard, God also bearing witness with them, both by signs and wonders and by various miracles and by gifts of the Holy Spirit according to His own will.* (**Hebrews 2:1-4**)

Not only has God spoken, but we must pay attention to what He said because our salvation from future, eternal judgment hangs in the balance! There is no indication that God's word was vague, unclear, cryptic, or subject to multiple meanings. If we neglect it we certainly shall not escape.

The Bible contains other indications that biblical writers considered its words clear, meaningful, and able to be understood. Jesus said this: "*He who rejects Me, and does not receive My sayings, has one who judges him; the word I spoke is what will judge him at the last day*" (**John 12:48**). When I cited this passage in my debate with Doug Pagitt it served a dual purpose–it refuted his idea that there is no literal, future judgment and it refuted his idea that the Bible cannot be fully understood. The challenge was necessary because if words are inadequate to convey meaning, then they are certainly inadequate to serve as grounds for eternal punishment. That denial had to be refuted.

Many biblical passages assert certainty. For example, Jesus said "*The Scripture cannot be broken*" (**John 10:35b**). He also said, "*But it is easier for heaven and earth to pass away than for one stroke of a letter of the Law to fail*" (**Luke 16:17**). Often the Gospels state that specific events happened "that the Scripture may be fulfilled."[148] And Jesus rebuked

148 See Luke 4:21; John 13:18; John 17:2; John 19:24, 28, 36; Matthew 26:54, 56; Mark 14:49

people for not understanding the Scriptures (**Mark 12:24**) when they ought to have understood them.

The apostles made careful arguments from the Old Testament Scriptures showing that they believed the Scriptures could be known and interpreted objectively. For example, in Romans 4:3-7 Paul argued from Genesis 15:6 that Abraham was declared righteous on the grounds of faith and that this declaration came before he was circumcised. Paul was engaged in objective exegesis that presupposed that the meaning of the Bible was clear and understandable. Paul engaged in debate based on the meaning of Scripture; "*[H]e powerfully refuted the Jews in public, demonstrating by the Scriptures that Jesus was the Christ* (**Acts 18:28**). If Luther's idea that the gospel of justification by faith could be known and that he could "stand" on it, was Luther inventing modernity as McLaren suggests? If so, Paul must have occupied "modernity" well before Luther's time: *Now I make known to you, brethren, the gospel which I preached to you, which also you received, in which also you stand,* (**1Corinthians 15:1**). Paul went on to cite eyewitness evidence for the veracity of the gospel.

Without further belaboring the point that the Biblical writers believed the Scriptures conveyed God's truth to man in a morally binding way, we must ask why those in the Emergent movement feel free to ignore what the Bible says about itself. Part of the answer lies in their previously discussed rejection of systematic theology. Previously, if one was going to reject doctrines such as the inerrancy of Scripture, the infallibility of Scripture, or the clarity of Scripture, one felt compelled to give good Biblical reasons for doing so. For example, if the Scriptures are not infallible, why did Jesus say that "*not one stroke of a letter of the Law could fail*"? Previously theologians would have to try to do some kind of exegetical wrangling to remove the obvious meaning of the passage. But the postmodern approach is to stay in the ethereal world of philosophical speculation for the most part and not even address the passages that obviously would refute their ideas. The earlier approach said that if one could not muster a solid argument based on sound Biblical exegesis of the most pertinent passages to validate a theological idea, the person would not be taken seriously. This is no longer the case—at least in some circles.

EMERGENT PREACHING

Interpreting the Bible according to Emergent/postmodern standards will affect preaching. Previously, preachers were expected to ground their sermons first and foremost in exegesis based on sound hermeneutics. The meaning of each passage was known to be determined by the Holy Spirit-inspired Biblical author, and any preaching not based on the meaning was invalid. This meant that Bible-believing preachers could declare with certainty what God has said and bind themselves and their listeners to valid application and implication of the text. This understanding of preaching is loathsome to the minds of most Emergent writers and thinkers.

Barry Taylor's contribution to *An Emergent Manifesto of Hope* rejects certainty about spiritual truth, considering it as dead as Neitzsche's "god."[149] Taylor writes, "Traditional faiths of every kind are experiencing challenges to their hegemony, to their claims on the truth, and to their self-proclaimed right to speak authoritatively on behalf of God."[150] Taking postmodern cultural development as not to be something to resist, Taylor calls for converting Christianity to something more like the culture itself; he calls it a "reverse conversion."[151] The new reality with the old "God" dead (we explored his credo, "God is nowhere, God is now here" in chapter one) must create a conversion process were the old Christianity becomes the new undefined spirituality. "In considering the future of Christian faith in the twenty-first century, I find this idea of reverse conversion to be really helpful," states Taylor.[152]

Obviously this rules out authoritative Bible preaching that presents "the faith once for all delivered to the saints" (Jude 3) because to him, rigid categories are unacceptable. His concept also rules out confronting the pagan culture with the changeless claims of Christ. The new "reality" is unending uncertainty. Consider his analysis:

> Religions exist in certainty and sanctity; faith lives in inquiry and fluidity. The reason traditional faiths are having a hard time is that the present situation

149 Barry Taylor, "Converting Christianity - The End and Beginning of Faith," in *Emergent Manifesto* 165.

150 Ibid.

151 Ibid. 169.

152 Ibid.

> is one in which certainty is suspect and sanctity is being redefined. We should consider letting go of our obsession with certainty . . . The future does not lie in the declaration of certainties, but in the living out of uncertainty."[153]

To give this claim the appearance of legitimacy he cites Paul saying that we "see through a glass darkly." But Paul was not speaking against the clarity of Scripture, but about "now" and the eschatological "then" when we shall be face to face with Christ. That is hugely different from denying the certainty of what God has revealed.

If we cannot proclaim Biblical truths as certain due to a reverse conversion process whereby Christianity finds a new "god" who is "now here," what are we to do? Taylor has a plan: "The future of Christian faith lies in its ability to inhabit this gray world, not attempting to 'sort it out' as much as to be available to help others navigate and negotiate the complexities that such a dynamic raises."[154] This, he says, is like the statement "go with the flow." He concludes with the idea that we need to find where God is in this fluid, uncertain process and what He is doing. How are we going to do that when we no longer accept any objective guidelines that reveal who God is, and what He has said?

Clearly, if we accept this view, Biblical proclamation of truth is dead. Satan's job will be much easier because he will not have to converse with anyone about what God said, because no one will have a clue what that might be; they will never hear it. If this agenda is followed, there will indeed have been a reverse conversion and the church shall be a mirror image of the pagan culture.

BIBLE PREACHING IN THE EMERGENT CHURCH

In his aptly titled book, *Preaching Re-imagined*, Pagitt directly addresses how the Bible is used in an Emergent Church. The book reveals the same tendencies we have been examining in this chapter. Pagitt creates a term, "speaching," which he uses to describe traditional Bible preaching as practiced by evangelicals: "The speacher decides the content ahead of time, usually in a removed setting, and then offers it in

153 Ibid. 168.
154 Ibid. 169.

such a way that the speacher is in control of the content, speed, and conclusion of the presentation."[155] Pagitt, like Taylor, dismisses those who make Biblical truths binding: "There is something dangerous in the life of the preacher who regularly tells others how things are, could be, or ought to be."[156]

We find out why Pagitt thinks it dangerous to speak from the Bible authoritatively:

> The contemporary church makes two mistakes regarding the function and relationship of the Bible. One is to think of her [remember, Pagitt refers to the Bible "she" and "her"] as a stagnant telling of all the desires of God. The other is to think of her as something from which we extract truth, whether in the form of moral teaching or propositional statements.[157]

Like neo-orthodox thinking of the previous century, and like the postmodern theologians discussed earlier in this chapter, Pagitt gives the appearance of elevating the status of the Bible by making "her" to be a living thing: "Progressional dialogue creates a relationship in which the Bible becomes a living member of the community."[158] As we shall see, this again means that the reader determines the meaning of scripture and that its meaning was not determined, once for all, by the Biblical writers.

Progressional dialogue is a group process that may go in several and varied directions: "Progressional dialogue, on the other hand, involves the intentional interplay of multiple viewpoints that leads to unexpected and unforeseen ideas. The message will change depending on who is present and who says what."[159] My problem is not in discussing the Bible, but with the contention that no singular meaning of the passage is determined by the Holy Spirit-inspired author. Without that and a hermeneutic that yields understanding of that meaning, we are

---

155 Doug Pagitt, *Preaching Re-imagined – The Role of the Sermon in Communities of Faith* (Grand Rapids: Zondervan, 2005) 22.

156 Ibid. 32.

157 Ibid. 44.

158 Ibid.

159 Ibid. 52.

back in the Garden with a conversation leading ever further away from what God said.

Pagitt's approach is merely another version of the hermeneutic that claims that the reader determines the meaning of the passage. Rather than to have someone make a Scriptural truth claim and the others judging whether or not the claim is valid based on Scripture (such as the Bereans), the group becomes the determiner of the meaning and not the recipient of it.

I believe that every Christian should be equipped to know and properly interpret the Scripture. I also believe that pastors who make false claims or misinterpret Scripture must listen to church members who correct them Biblically. Pastors have no ecclesiastical power to determine the meaning of the Bible. That is why the Reformation stood on the credo, "*sola scriptura*."

But Pagitt is taking this an entirely different direction by assuming that the Holy Spirit is guiding the group process to some truth not controlled by the Biblical author:

> The people of God, in communion with the Bible and the Holy Spirit, have the truth of God within them. That is, the story of God helps us interpret the reality with which we interact. The Holy Spirit guides this interaction and interpretation. Every person has experience, understanding, and perspective; there is no one who is totally devoid of truth.[160]

One has to ask, then, would not this process work just as well with some other book? The only reason to think not is tantamount to attributing magical quality to the Bible that causes it to influence the group through some means other than its authoritative content. But how do we know some other book would not work better?

It is also troubling that Pagitt assumes those who believe in the authoritative proclamation of Biblical truth have bad motives. He sees at the heart of Biblical preaching a desire to control others (again, he calls it "speaching"). Here is his *ad hominem* argument:

160 Ibid. 139.

> At the heart of the resistance to progressional dialogue as a legitimate method of preaching is the question of control. The speaching act allows for the preacher not only to control the content, but also to apply the sermon to people's lives. In basketball there is an expression for a person who does everything on the court—get the rebound, dribble up the court, and shoot. This person is called a ball hog, and no one likes having one on the court.[161]

How does he know that only those with bad motives preach sermons? It must be possible, and very likely, that some of us believe that God has commanded us to preach the gospel. Maybe we actually believe that people will come to saving faith if confronted with the truth of the gospel. Maybe we believe that God uses the truth of His Word to sanctify Christians. But Pagitt says pastors might, "[E]ven have the gall to think they can apply messages they create to the lives of other people."[162]

In this Emergent way of thinking, other dangers exist when preaching God's word: "This effort to maintain control over a centralized message naturally lead to a centralized understanding of God."[163] Since the world is pluralistic and fluid we must adjust in the following way: "Being part of a global, pluralistic world is a great gift to the church, for our role in ministry is not to push the agenda of our clan but to recognize and join in the life of God wherever we find it."[164] This brings us right back to the same conundrum: we have no objective basis or means to know what is or is not the "life of God," but we have to find that life and join it.

ALL PATHS LEAD TO GOD?

Ironically, the Serpent told Eve that she would find god-like life by ignoring the clear teaching of God's Word and developing her own ideas about it in dialogue. In the Emergent conversation the Biblical

161 Ibid. 123.
162 Ibid.
163 Ibid. 125.
164 Ibid.

writers' meaning is deemed unknowable, and neither did they determine the meaning. Instead, they believe that communities of readers determine their own meaning, that there is no objective way to know whether or not the meaning one interpretive community gave to the Bible is any closer to truth than that of another. They teach that the kingdom of God (or the life of God) is discovered in the world through a process of looking for it, except that there are no objective means of distinguishing what is or is not from God other than pragmatic tests which cannot be used to discover eternal truth.

Given such an understanding of the Bible, it is no wonder that they deem the proclamation of truth to be an offense to postmodern sensibilities as well as the fact that all ideas—whatever they might be—are to be given equal opportunity in order to be found "true for me". How could such a process be deemed "hope"? We are brought right back to the eschatological underpinning of Emergent/postmodern thinking: "God is the future drawing everything toward Himself." In their worldview, since all paths ultimately lead to God, they know that their conversation will land them with God in paradise—as will all other conversations.

Abstract Chapter 6

Undefining the Means of Grace

MEANS OF GRACE—HOW WE APPROACH GOD AND GROW IN SANCTIFICATION

The term "means of grace" is used to define how we come to God and by what processes we grow in sanctification and conformity to the image of His Son. Because Emergent rejects boundaries and definitions, we observe a diverse "freestyle" approach to the means of grace where every person, or at least every congregation, designs for themselves what measures they take to approach God. While they may be diverse in their methods, the Emergent pursue mysticism—spiritual experiences—in order to come to God and grow spiritually. Since recorded history, and even before, mystical spiritual experiences have been the method by which humanity has employed in its attempts to approach God; it is commonly known as paganism. Just as the Emergent is diverse, paganism is equally diverse—with as many "means of grace" as there are tribes and people groups—and they all believe they are approaching God.

SETTING ASIDE SCRIPTURE, PRAYER, AND BIBLE TEACHING FOR NEO-PAGAN PRACTICES

Early "Christians" who sought methods in order to achieve spiritual experiences with their "Christian" God adopted pagan mystical practices. These destructive practices influenced the Catholic Church and led to its decay. (It also led to the Reformation.) The Emergent have embraced these ancient, destructive practices, re-labeled them as "spiritual disciplines," and reintroduced them into the Protestant Evangelical church as "lost secrets" of spirituality. Instead of studying the scripture in order to understand Jesus, His will, and His character, then praying that the Holy Spirit would conform us to His image, the Emergent pursuit focuses on "spiritual formation" in order to grow in spiritual experiences. In contrast, Christianity is the belief as literal history that Jesus Christ—a human being who was equally God—lived, died, and was raised from the dead. And real human beings recorded it as such in an actual book. He bodily ascended into heaven and awaits His return. When we believe that this sinless man's death paid the price for our sins and that through His death we are reconciled to God, we really can approach God the Father with confidence and offer our petitions to Him in prayer. As we study and grow in our belief concerning the life and person of Jesus Christ, and what He did for us, we change and become more like Him.

6

Undefining the Means of Grace

The Word of God is the primary means of grace by which God converts the lost and sanctifies the redeemed. It is the preaching of the gospel that converts the lost who believe. Those who are thus converted are sanctified as they are taught the pure Word of God. But the Emergent/postmodern understanding of Scripture means that there is no authoritative gospel even to preach. A resultant corollary is that the Bible no longer serves as a means to conform lives into the image of Christ.

How, may we ask, are lives changed according to the Emergent Church? The answer is by any means a given Emergent community determines to work for them. Rather than practicing God's ordained means of grace revealed in the Bible, a religious community experiments to determine its practices. By all accounts, these experiments lead in many directions. But one direction most of them have in common is this: mysticism.

PRACTICES WITHOUT BOUNDARIES

Earlier we used logical categories to prove the legitimacy of boundaries and to show that human reason is not possible without them. Concerning God's means of grace, the removal of boundaries opens the door to pagan practices. This happens because pagans have contrived their own spirituality throughout human history. In some cases they have become very adept at contacting the spirit world in order to hear voices that they imagine are from God or the gods. Those who are best at this become gurus or shamans.

During the middle ages, Roman Catholicism also developed spiritual practices not prescribed in the Bible. By definition, practices God did not prescribe (those designed to contact God or enhance one's spirituality) can only be judged on a pragmatic basis: "it works for me so it must be good". Because what is or is not "biblical" has been ruled out before the discussion begins, the emergent community, by definition, has accepted only pragmatic boundaries for its practices. This is shown in the continual theme that orthopraxy (correct practice) is more important than orthodoxy. But, since there is no authoritative word from God to define one's practices (according to emergent/postmodern thinking), the term "orthopraxy" is as meaningless as "orthodoxy" in their world.

Many examples of this thinking are contained among the essays of *An Emergent Manifesto of Hope*. For example, Mark Scandrette writes, "Our constructions of faith and practice are dismantled and, at times, destroyed so that we can approximate a more coherent and integrative *orthopraxis*—good theology and good living."[165] This could be considered valid if it meant that we have an authoritative Bible whose meaning can be known in a non-relativistic way and based on that meaning we "dismantled" unbiblical practices in order to institute Biblical ones. That was the idea of the Reformation. But for these Emergent writers, that idea is a relic of the Enlightenment quest for certainty. Therefore, we have no authoritative blueprint with which to compare our building plans to see if they are in keeping with God's intention. The Bible calls that "building on sand" (see Matthew 7:24-27).

Not having a once-for-all revealed faith, but rather a process in history imagined to be guided by the Spirit, they are left with experimentation:

165 Mark Scandrette, "Growing Pains - The Messy and Fertile Process of Becoming," in *An Emergent Manifesto of Hope* Doug Pagitt and Tony Jones editors (Grand Rapids: Baker, 2007) 26.

> In terms of God's agenda to remake and restore all of creation, "good news" is something that is as much inhabited as it is believed. Therefore, how we live is of equal importance to what we believe or how we practice the rituals of a particular community or tradition. This allows for an experimental approach to the Christian faith and practice.[166]

Such an approach is entirely hopeless because we live in a world of spiritual deception. If God has spoken once for all, as the Biblical writers claimed, then why must we search the world looking for practices we deem better than the Biblically prescribed ones? Emergent writers routinely accuse people like me of being naïve foundationalists who have no clue that our imagined certainty about knowing the truth is based on rationalistic presuppositions not valid in the postmodern world. But I counter that their naïveté is much greater. They assume that they can experiment with religious practices and not be deceived by the spirits that have for centuries been betraying pagans who employ the same practices. What is more naïve—to think we can know the meaning of the God-breathed Bible, which was written in human language, or to think that by using pagan practices we can enter the world of deceptive spirits and emerge with something closer to the Kingdom of God on earth? The question is rhetorical, but I believe my point is clear.

Scandrette sees hope nearly everywhere, even in the thinking of neo-pagan, New Age advocates:

> Perhaps interest in theologies of the kingdom of God is related to the contemporary quest for holism, integration, and a sense of interconnection. My colleague, Dr. Linda Bergquist, has suggested that renewed popularity of the "kingdom" language is related to the emerging global narrative of the deep ecology movement—a consciousness and

166 Ibid.

> awareness that everything matters and is somehow interdependent.[167]

The deep ecology movement sees traditional Christianity's understanding of man's uniqueness (as created in God's image and given authority over the earth) as a terrible cause of the earth's problems. Instead it finds its thinking from pagan sources and a decidedly pagan worldview that values the "interconnectedness of all things," including the "Gaia hypothesis."[168] Of course, this pagan idea runs contrary to a Biblical worldview.

Brian McLaren describes his experience with this type of interconnectedness:

> I felt that every tree, every blade of grass, and every pool of water become especially eloquent with God's grandeur. Somehow they seemed to become transparent—or perhaps *translucent* is the better word—because each thing in its particularity was still utterly visible and unspeakably important . . . These specific, concrete things became translucent in the sense that a powerful, indescribable, invisible light seemed to shine through. . . . It was the exuberant joy of simply seeing these masterpieces of God's creation...and knowing myself to be among them. It was to be one of them, and to feel and know that "we"—all of these creatures, molecules, and phenomena—were together known and loved by God, who embraced us all into the ultimate "We."[169]

This underscores the danger of basing Christian belief and practice on experience without holding an *a priori* understanding of truth based scriptural revelation. McLaren's experience, I conclude, is something deceptive that would lead toward a New Age or neo-pagan understanding of the world. It is panentheistic.

167 Ibid. 27.

168 http://www.webnb.btinternet.co.uk/deep.htm#_Toc482714833 (Accessed December, 2007).

169 Brian D. McLaren, *a Generous Orthodoxy* (Grand Rapids: Zondervan, 2004) 178.

When we erase boundaries in hope of finding an emerging kingdom, we are led away from the biblically described means of grace and toward practices and beliefs cherished by pagan society. Scandrette says, "We see this longing for integrative theology and practice expressed in various themes within the emerging church phenomenon." He then gives a list that includes, among other things, communal living, monastic practices, "open-source" approach to theology, global justice and advocacy, contemplative and bodily spiritual formation disciplines, creation theology that celebrates earth, cultures and the sensuous, and provocative storytelling.[170] Scandrette himself is involved with monasticism: "As a monastic community we experiment with common life rhythms inspired by Jesus's example."[171]

"SPIRITUAL FORMATION" IS NOT SANCTIFICATION

Scandrette mentioned "contemplative and bodily spiritual formation" as thematic in many emergent communities. These terms do not denote the Biblical doctrine of sanctification based on the blood atonement and the continued work of grace whereby God works through His ordained means to progressively conform all true believers into the image of Christ (Romans 8:29, 30). The sanctification process is completed at the resurrection. Spiritual formation is something entirely different. Spiritual formation is the process by which people use various "disciplines" designed to make them feel closer to God and to have a greater sense of inner peace. The heroes of the spiritual formation movement often are Catholic mystics like Henri Nouwen and Thomas Merton, and teachers like Richard Foster and Dallas Willard. These men have sold these ideas to unsuspecting evangelicals.

For example, Dan Kimball is a well known Emergent pastor whose book *The Emerging Church – Vintage Christianity for New Generations* contains endorsements of various mystical writers such as Henri Nouwen, John Michael Talbot (a Roman Catholic mystic), and Dallas Willard. [172] For Kimball, "vintage Christianity" means teaching non-biblical practices from the medieval Roman Catholic Church. Kim-

---

170 Scandrette, 27, 28.

171 Ibid.

172 Dan Kimball, *The Emergent Church – Vintage Christianity for New Generations* (Grand Rapids: Zondervan, 2003) 257, 258.

ball laments, "We have neglected so many of the disciplines of the historical church, including weekly fasting, practicing silence, and *lectio divina*."[173] Well known evangelical Chip Ingram makes a side bar comment in Kimball's book endorsing what Kimball says about the disciplines.

Do not be deceived; no such "spiritual disciplines" are found in the Bible. God Himself has ordained for all Christians the means of grace. The "disciplines" are discovered by spiritual innovators who think they can blaze their own spiritual trails. For example, *lectio divina* is a practice that ignores the meaning of the Biblical authors and instead seeks a personal revelation or spiritual experience from a word that supposedly will spring out of context, off the page to the practitioner of that particular discipline. Here is how a current Roman Catholic teacher describes it:

> A VERY ANCIENT art, practiced at one time by all Christians, is the technique known as *lectio divina* - a slow, contemplative praying of the Scriptures which enables the Bible, the Word of God, to become a means of union with God. This ancient practice has been kept alive in the Christian monastic tradition, and is one of the precious treasures of Benedictine monastics and oblates. Together with the Liturgy and daily manual labor, time set aside in a special way for *lectio divina* enables us to discover in our daily life an underlying spiritual rhythm. Within this rhythm we discover an increasing ability to offer more of ourselves and our relationships to the Father, and to accept the embrace that God is continuously extending to us in the person of his Son Jesus Christ.[174]

This practice has nothing to do with the Word of God as a means of grace. Moreover, the biblical passage is merely a means of creating a spiritual experience unrelated to the meaning of the text.

---

173 Ibid. 223.

174 http://www.valyermo.com/ld-art.html Fr. Luke Dysinger, O.S.B. (accessed December 26, 2007).

A student of a local Baptist Bible College recently gave me a book by Richard Foster which was required reading for a course on "Spiritual Disciplines." Authors of the essays in the book include many mystics such as Thomas Merton, Dallas Willard, Henri Nouwen, Madame Guyon, and others, mixed in with essays from others holding orthodox theology. Madame Guyon's portion shows that the mystics do not concern themselves with the meaning of the Bible. She wrote, "In the past it may have been your habit, while reading, to move very quickly from one verse of Scripture to another until you have read the whole passage. Perhaps you were seeking to find the main point of the passage."[175] But the author's meaning is of no concern in such practices, so it is not surprising that the Emergent/postmodern approach favors these practices; they do not believe the meaning of the Biblical authors can be known.

Guyon continues her description of the mystical approach to reading the Bible:

> Therefore, as you come before the Lord to sit in his presence, beholding him, make use of the Scripture to *quiet* your mind. The way to do this is really quite simple. First, read a passage of Scripture. Once you sense the Lord's presence, the content of what you read is no longer important. The Scripture has served its purpose; it has quieted your mind; it has brought you to him.[176]

This is the problem: if we pay no attention to the terms of Scripture that indicate how to come to God and how to determine the true God from the deceiving spirits, we cannot know that a specific experience gained from a quieted mind is God Himself or a demon sent by Satan to deceive practitioners of this sort of divination. A person could invoke the same experience by using any book as long as he was convinced the book had some magical qualities.

---

175 Madame Guyon, excerpts from "Experiencing the Depths of Jesus Christ," in *Devotional Classics*, Richard Foster and James Bryan Smith editors, (New York: HarperCollins, 1993) 320.
176 Ibid. 321.

Doug Pagitt claims that we can become closer to God through various postures he and others have discovered in a book entitled *Body Prayer – The Posture of Intimacy With God*.[177] Please take careful note: in each of these claims we are called upon to decide whether God has revealed how we come to Him and the means by which He promises to sanctify us or whether we are free to invent an approach according to our own determination—and expect God to honor it. As became evident in our 2006 debate, I believe God reveals such things and has drawn the boundaries for our practices and Pagitt takes the free-style approach. He shows his proclivity to the freestyle approach, as other Emergent leaders do, by endorsing ancient, unbiblical practices: "People of faith in ancient times understood such physical acts and practices as rest and worship, dietary restrictions, and mandated fabric in their wardrobes were of great value to their faith and life."[178] The Bible warns against such approaches in Colossians 2. Where do we get the right to ignore what God has said and glean our practices from spiritual innovators? Pagitt continues, "Similarly, walking a prayer labyrinth, going on pilgrimage, and making the sign of the cross have served to connect the physical body to the life of faith through the centuries."[179]

In the spirit of unbiblical Roman Catholic innovations, Pagitt and co-author Kathryn Prill have created their own means of drawing near to God. They promise this about their "prayer postures": "Bodyprayer is designed to help you connect with God at every level of your life—body, mind and spirit."[180] The book is filled with various postures to practice. One in particular is called "stepping forward" which signifies stepping into the rhythm of God:

> And there is a rhythm to God—a rhythm that encompasses life, both the life we can readily see and the unseen life of the spirit. The rhythm of God beckons us, guides us, and dwells in us. When we discover the rhythm of God, we find the heart of God,

177 Doug Pagitt and Kathryn Prill, *Body Prayer – The Posture of Intimacy With God* (Colorado Springs: WaterBrook Press, 2005).

178 Ibid. 3.

179 Ibid. 4.

180 Ibid. 7.

> the dreams of God, the will of God. As those who are created in the image of God, we are endowed with this rhythm. We can find it, step into it, and live in it. This is the kingdom of God—to live in sync with the rhythm of God.[181]

This mystical theology is a denial of the fallen nature of man and suggests that all humans can find God by discovering this undefined "rhythm" within them. The gospel says that we are dead sinners, alienated from God who can only be reconciled to God through the work of redemption that Jesus Christ provided on the cross. The "rhythms" that speak outside of Christ's objective work revealed in the gospel are deceiving spirits who seduce people into thinking they are finding the "kingdom" apart from repentance and submission to the revealed will of the King!

FINDING HOLINESS AND DRAWING NEAR TO GOD

The issue of holiness is very important in the Bible. In the Old Testament, God set up requirements and stringent barriers because He, the holy God, dwelt in the midst of His people. One of those barriers was the curtain that kept separate the Most Holy Place. The high priest could only enter there once per year on the Day of Atonement—and only if he kept the stipulations for preparation according to God's revealed Law. The book of Hebrews takes up this theme, revealing that God has made provisions by which humans may draw near to Him.

The need for holiness in order draw near to the Holy God of the Bible is still real. But the good news is that we have a High Priest who provides everything we need for drawing near to God:

> *The former priests, on the one hand, existed in greater numbers because they were prevented by death from continuing, but Jesus, on the other hand, because He continues forever, holds His priesthood permanently. Therefore He is able also to save forever those who draw near to God through Him, since He always lives to make intercession for them. For it was fitting for us to have such a high priest, holy, innocent, undefiled,*

181 Ibid. 127.

> *separated from sinners and exalted above the heavens; who does not need daily, like those high priests, to offer up sacrifices, first for His own sins and then for the sins of the people, because this He did once for all when He offered up Himself.* (**Hebrews 7:23-27**)

Jesus Christ, our High Priest, shed his own blood once for all to provide a way for us to draw near to God—and we must trust in Him. And without holiness, no one will see the Lord (**Hebrews 12:14**). Those who neglect Christ's blood atonement remain in their own sinful, defiled condition, and they face God as judge rather than savior.

The central issue in Hebrews is faith in what Christ has provided once for all, rather to return to Old Covenant practices that had been done away with. This issue was so serious that Hebrews contains many dire warnings against apostasy. For example: "*Anyone who has set aside the Law of Moses dies without mercy on the testimony of two or three witnesses. How much severer punishment do you think he will deserve who has trampled under foot the Son of God, and has regarded as unclean the blood of the covenant by which he was sanctified, and has insulted the Spirit of grace?*" (**Hebrews 10:28, 19**) God determines terms of the covenant, and those who transgress them have nothing to look forward to but "*a certain terrifying expectation of judgment*" (**Hebrews 10:27**). To look elsewhere other than to the blood of Christ (averting God's wrath against our sin for means to draw near to God) is to regard the blood of the covenant as "unclean" and insult the Holy Spirit!

Why would anyone be motivated to put themselves in such peril? The answer is found through faith. Faith is the conviction of things not seen (**Hebrews 11:1**). The Hebrew Christians lived when the temple sacrifices were still in operation (**Hebrews 8:13**). Everything important concerning the New Covenant—other than the written Word, the elements of the Lord's Supper, and the water of baptism—is unseen. This includes the tabernacle and its mercy seat and other fixtures, which are in heaven (**Hebrews 9:11, 24**) and thus unseen. The blood is unseen, the High Priest is unseen, and the blood cleanses the unseen conscience rather than the seen flesh (**Hebrews 9:13, 14**). The mountain that could be touched (**Hebrews 12:18**) that was ablaze with a theophany of God is not comparable to the intangible things that New Covenant believers have come to:

> *But you have come to Mount Zion and to the city of the living God, the heavenly Jerusalem, and to myriads of angels, to the general assembly and church of the first-born who are enrolled in heaven, and to God, the Judge of all, and to the spirits of righteous men made perfect, and to Jesus, the mediator of a new covenant, and to the sprinkled blood, which speaks better than the blood of Abel.* (**Hebrews 12:22 – 24**)

The contrast between the seen and tangible (either now or in Israel's past) and the unseen and intangible is found throughout Hebrews.

The Hebrew Christians were tempted to apostatize because of a failure of faith analogous to that of their forefathers in the wilderness. Once Moses was out of sight the wilderness Israelites said, "*Come, make us a god who will go before us; as for this Moses, the man who brought us up from the land of Egypt, we do not know what has become of him.*" (**Exodus 32:1b**) Moses had become unseen so the golden calf became a more tangible representative of God. Likewise, the high priest in Jerusalem could be seen in his glorious attire, the blood of the sacrifices could be seen and the burnt offerings could be smelled, so the Jews could go back to the old covenant and enjoy the experience with all five senses. But what Christianity offered was unseen. It could only be "seen" through the eyes of faith; so there was great temptation to apostatize.

The issue of drawing near to God in the Emergent Church is identical. Only biblical Christianity offers belief that one may be made holy and able to draw near to the Holy God who is in heaven. It is a belief based on tangible evidence found in history. Jesus ascended to heaven after he died and rose again. We must believe the apostolic witnesses to this event (Hebrews 2:3, 4) under pain of neglecting our salvation and coming under judgment. But having determined that the Holy Spirit-inspired words in the Bible cannot be known well enough to validate anything, the Emergent Church has chosen the path Hebrews warns against: to worship using all five senses in a way that seems more tangible than to believe God's Word. Why draw near to the throne of grace in prayer (Hebrews 4:16) when we cannot even know it exists other than by faith?

The Roman Catholic Church tried to create tangibility for worshipers with all manner of holy objects, icons, saints, sights, and smells. This happened when the church, through conquest, forced illiterate pagans into the church. The church leaders did not expect these worshippers to know the Bible and live by faith in God's word. Instead, the leaders offered the pagan communicants "faith" that the church leaders had things "right" as well as the tangibility of icon-filled cathedrals. Now the Emergent Church is going in the same direction, not because of massive illiteracy, but because of the post-modern angst about the ability to communicate with words.

DRAWING NEAR TO GOD THROUGH YOGA

Everywhere we look in the Emergent church we see the desire for a more tangible way to approach God. Consider the idea of being "abductive" found in *A is for Abductive – The Language of the Emerging Church*: "Before asking yourself before creating a sermon, 'What's my point?' ask yourself 'What's my image?' or in more musical terms, 'What experience do I want to compose.'"[182] The idea is this: Do not seek to convince people with facts and evidence–seek to pull them into a new world for them to experience. But, as we saw in Hebrews, the world of redemption is based on matters that are only accessible by faith, and not by tangible experience. Abduction means to "Seize people by the imagination and transport them from their current world to another world, where they gain a new perspective."[183] Teaching the Bible and calling people to believe its truth claims simply will not create the right experience for abductees. Instead one must use "Disorientation, astonishment, amazement . . . you beam them up into the spaceship of an unexpected experience."[184]

When the boundaries between God-ordained practices and pagan practices are erased, as is the case in the Emergent Church, then it makes sense to find practices that are attractive to people in

182 Leonard Sweet, Brian McLaren, and Jerry Haselmayer, *A is for Abductive – The Language of the Emerging Church* (Grand Rapids: Zondervan, 2003) 31, 32.

183 Ibid. 31.

184 Ibid. 32.

the surrounding culture. One such practice is Yoga. Although Yoga is a Hindu practice and intimately related to various Hindu deities, some Christians have begun to bring this pagan practice into the Church. Some claim that they have removed any religious content and are merely using Yoga positions for exercise. But this is wrong and dangerous. In the case of Pagitt's church, Solomon's Porch, Yoga clearly is not merely "exercise."

Pagitt's book, *Church Re-imagined*, contains a description of the church's weekly yoga class written by the woman who leads it.[185] She states, "We aren't here for a hardcore physical workout as much as the chance to be together, to breathe, to relax, and to bring ourselves to a place of peace and gratitude."[186] The process includes having the students regulate their breathing. They also use different poses each week: "These vary from week to week, but Downward Facing Dog is a must."[187] The poses and breathing are designed to do something to their inner state: "This [that the chit-chat has stopped] tells me that tension has been released from the muscles, inner chatter has moved out of the brain, and self-awareness and peacefulness have settled in."[188]

The yoga instructor gives a more detailed description of the last pose:

> Our last pose of the evening is called "savasana" . . . or corpse pose. The student lies on her back letting the legs fall open as they will, the arms hang limp like empty coat sleeves. The face, the forehead, the space between the eyebrows all relax, and the person melts heavily into the floor. Eyes are closed, breathing is rhythmic. I turn the lights off, and only the glow of candles and sometimes fireplace illuminates the room. This state of being is holy. It is at this time that

185 Doug Pagitt, *Church Re-Imagined – The Spiritual Formation of People in Communities of Faith* (Grand Rapids: Zondervan, 2005) 85.

186 Ibid.

187 Ibid.

188 Ibid. 87.

> we become closer to God, aware of our bodies, of the divine.[189]

Clearly, her claim is that yoga is a means to become holy and draw near to God. A corollary to this claim is that humans have a right to determine their own path to God. The Bible makes it clear that we must come to God on His terms only, not ours! It is one thing to claim the right to use practices of other religions in a non-religious way (which I believe has no place in the church), but it is egregious to claim that practices from pagan religions can make us holy and closer to God.

This belief is known as "Interspirituality," an idea promoted by the late Catholic mystic Wayne Teasdale. Here is how Teasdale describes it:

> Interspirituality is a term to describe the breaking down of the barriers that have separated the religions for millennia. It is also the crossing-over and sharing in the spiritual, aesthetic, moral and psychological treasures that exist in the spiritualities of the world religions. The deepest level of sharing is in and through one another's mystical wisdom, whether teachings, insights, methods of spiritual practice and their fruits.[190]

Teasdale recognizes mysticism as a way to bring various world religions together. In a way he is probably correct, but in a most tragic sense.

In his excellent book, *A Time of Departing*, Ray Yungen claims that New Age mysticism outside and inside the church is setting up the entire world for the one-world religion of antichrist:

> Someday, and it could be soon, the Lord will allow the man of lawlessness to emerge. In the mean time,

189 Ibid. 87, 89.

190 Wayne Teasdale, *Mysticism as the Crossing of Ultimate Boundaries:* A Theological Reflection http://www.bedegriffiths.com/golden/gs_10.htm (accessed December 2007).

> the world is opening its arms to wholly embrace a spirituality that will exist under the umbrella of mysticism. The correlating theme will be—we are all One. When the man of lawlessness does rise to power with a one-world economy and political base, he will seduce many into searching for their own *Christ consciousness* rather than the Messiah, Jesus Christ.[191]

Yoga, prayer labyrinths, contemplative prayer, and other expressions of mysticism in the Emerging Church constitute supposed pathways to God; but they are pathways that Christ called the "broad way" that leads to destruction (Matthew 7:13).

Back to Solomon's Porch and the yoga class that purports to make people holy and close to God. The yoga instructor says this about the end of a class: "I stand to switch on a lamp. Slowly people get up, talk, commit to a daily practice of yoga in hopes of getting this feeling again and again. We are hesitant to leave this moment of shared reverence, this experience of worship."[192] The operative word here is "experience." We have shown that coming to God on His terms requires faith. As we saw in Hebrews, the danger is that we depart from the faith to seek a tangible religious experience rather than simply to believe the unseen God in heaven and obey His commands. Simply because the yoga took place in a church building, it is no proof that it was the God of the Bible who provided the experience. God has set boundaries for our faith and practices; yoga is outside of those boundaries. And I told that to Pastor Pagitt in our debate.

When we teach as a means of worship what is not revealed by God we are indulging in what Jesus calls "vain worship": "*But in vain do they worship Me, Teaching as doctrines the precepts of men*" (**Mark 7:7**). Because yoga is not prescribed by authoritative spokespersons for God (the Biblical writers), it falls into the category of "vain worship."

---

191 Ray Yungen, *A Time of Departing – How Ancient Mystical Practices are Uniting Christians with the World's Religions*; (Silverton, Or.: Lighthouse Trails, 2nd edition 2006) 127, 128.

192 Pagitt, *Church*, 89.

God does not ordain freestyle, mystical experiences. Teasdale explains how he understood mystical experiences, such as those who use Eastern mystical approaches:

> On the mystical level there is an option between an intimate, personal, loving God, with whom we can enter into a profound relationship of love and knowledge in the embrace of divine union initiated by God, or the transpersonal, impersonal realization of the ultimate condition of mind or consciousness, of the Buddhist tradition. Both these trajectories of mystical perception are available to us. Perhaps it is necessary for us to experience both of these ways, and that is what interspirituality challenges us to do.[193]

McLaren as well suggests that Christianity has things to learn from other religions: "Western Christianity has (for the last few centuries anyway) said relatively little about mindfulness and meditative practices, about which Zen Buddhism has said much. To talk about different things is not to contradict one another; it is rather, to have much to offer one another, on occasion at least."[194] The Emergent Church has indeed learned much from Eastern religions, particularly mysticism.

WHAT ABOUT DECEIVING SPIRITS?

We began our look at the Emerging Church by describing its eschatology originally articulated by Jürgen Moltmann. Once again, the reason they attach the term "hope" to Emergent/postmodern theology is found in the eschatological idea that God is in the future, pulling everything toward Himself. The paradoxes and contradictions will, according to this thinking, be synthesized into a better reality until that reality ultimately becomes the full manifestation of the Kingdom of God on earth.

One subject I found lacking, however, as I read Shults, Moltmann, Grenz, and their Emergent theological followers, is Satan and

193 Teasdale, *Mysticism.*

194 McLaren, *Generous,* 255.

deceiving spirits. In the Bible God articulates the means of grace objectively. God spoke through His ordained apostles and prophets and revealed the terms of salvation from sin and the means of growing in the grace and knowledge of the Lord Jesus Christ. Likewise, in the Old Testament, God spoke through Moses and objectively revealed the terms by which the people must come to God and faithfully serve Him. According to Deuteronomy 18, any other practices are forbidden. What lies outside of God's self-revelation is the realm of spirits: "*There shall not be found among you anyone who makes his son or his daughter pass through the fire, one who uses divination, one who practices witchcraft, or one who interprets omens, or a sorcerer, or one who casts a spell, or a medium, or a spiritist, or one who calls up the dead*" (**Deuteronomy 18:10, 11**).

Furthermore, the New Testament warns about deceiving spirits and defines Satan as one whose nature is to lie (John 8:44). This being the case, why would anyone use practices not ordained in the Bible but contrived by practitioners of other religions—and then think that they have found God in the experience? I believe the answer is in their underlying theological presumptions. They have determined that the meaning of the Biblical authors is not assessable in a non relativistic way (as opposed to knowing God's absolute truth). Therefore it cannot prescribe practices. Furthermore, they have determined that the processes of history are being brought forward in a way that all paths lead to God in a saving way. They have assumed that the Holy Spirit is at work in their communities bringing them closer to God, although they refuse to apply the Biblical test of spirits (1John 4:1-5) to see if they are following the Holy Spirit or the deceiving spirits.

The result is that they lack the fear of being deceived by spirits. When they use breathing techniques or other means of altering their states of consciousness, whereby one is open to the world of spirits, their naïve assumption is that if the resulting experience makes one *feel* closer to God, the worshipper must therefore *be* closer to God. In the description of the yoga class in Pagitt's Emergent Church, there is no evidence that anyone considered the possibility that it was not the true God of the Bible they were encountering.

The way we know that it is God and not a deceiving spirit we encounter in our worship experience is whether or not we have come to him under the terms He has revealed once and for all. Confessing

"Jesus Christ come in the flesh" is John's shorthand way of saying confessing the complete doctrine of the Incarnation and its implications for salvation. The only way we can know it was truly Christ we met there is if we entered through the narrow gate. The only way we can know whether or not our religious practices are bringing us closer to God is if those practices are the ones God ordained in the Bible. Yoga was not ordained; therefore those practicing it are putting themselves into the spiritual realm by a means God does not approve of. Deceiving spirits occupy that realm and they are more than motivated to give such "worshippers" a wonderful, positive experience that makes them feel closer to God. Why? Because as long as they feel close to God through mysticism, these worshippers will never actually come to God through the gospel.

Tony Jones' "tractor beam of redemption" is not God pulling everyone toward a universally salvific future. Rather, it is the magnetism of deceiving spirits who have inhabited the spirit realm for many centuries, have nefarious plans for humans and are expert at giving people experiences that will keep them coming back for more. They are not pulling them toward salvation, but damnation. Sadly, the Emergent Church has no defense against these spirits because they have no authoritative Bible to guide them to true beliefs and practices where they would meet God on His terms.

In the next chapter we shall examine the non-foundational epistemology of postmodern theology and the Emergent Church. We shall see that their approach to knowledge leaves them detached from the real world.

=Abstract Chapter 7

Undefining Knowledge—The Epistemology of the Emergent Church

REMOVING THE FOUNDATIONS OF KNOWLEDGE AND TRUTH

Epistemology is the theory of knowledge, and it primarily addresses the following questions: "What is knowledge?" and "How is knowledge acquired?" Christianity believes knowledge of salvation and reconciliation with God is revealed in the Bible. Some Christians simply state that it is true because it is true (presuppositionists); and others believe it is true because it is historically accurate and is based on factual evidence (evidentialists). Both views agree that the scriptures are foundational for knowledge of salvation, of God, and of the world we live in.

COHERENTISM—SCIENCE FICTION "TRUTH" AND FANTASY "TRUTH"

Emergent rejects absolutes and a world of cause and effect, instead believing in a "socially constructed" world in which our beliefs create the "worlds" in which we live. According to Emergent, each individual or congregation may imagine their own world, and the only way to determine whether it is "true" or not is to determine whether that imagined world is consistent within itself. If it is consistent, then it is true and equally valid to someone else's world (regardless of whether these worlds contradict each other). The easiest way to understand this is to consider that each individual is a science fiction or fantasy writer creating a novel. As long as the world described in the novel is consistent with itself; it is enough. The fact that the world of *Lord of the Rings* does not agree with the world of the *Matrix* or of *Alice in Wonderland* matters not at all; what matters is that the world itself is coherent (coherentism).

LINKING OUR CONCEPT OF KNOWLEDGE TO THE REAL WORLD

While building worlds may be an interesting and creative exercise, the real issue regarding humanity and God is whether or not this world accurately reflects the reality we live in and the reality revealed in scripture. For Christians, imaginary worlds are not valuable concerning salvation and eternity; at best they are entertainment, and at worst (when they are believed) they are delusions that lead to damnation.

7

Undefining Knowledge—The Epistemology of the Emergent Church

The "demise of foundationalism" is a consistent theme among Emergent and postmodern writers. Foundationalism is an approach to knowledge that seeks to build a foundation for other beliefs based on certain "givens" or "basic" beliefs that are self-evident. The postmodern critics claim that the Enlightenment quest for certainty has failed and that we must rethink everything (including Christian theology) because we can no longer have certainty about truth claims. We discussed this issue in chapter 3, but now it is time to look more closely at the foundationalism they suppose has met its demise as well as the postmodern proposals offered as a replacement.

As I pointed out in chapter 3, evangelicals of a previous generation debated one another concerning evidentialist versus presuppositionist apologetics. I noted that both of these approaches were foundationalist and that both are considered equally antiquated in the current stream of postmodern thinking. The evidentialists believed that one could study evidence that Christ was raised from the dead in order to validate Christianity. Famous books such as *Who Moved the Stone* by Frank Morison set out to examine the evidence of Christianity's claim of the resurrection of Christ to prove it a myth.

But Morison found the historical evidence to be so compelling that he converted to Christianity.[195] If Christ was indeed raised, then His other claims are validated as well—other claims such as His being the Son of God, the Jewish Messiah, and God Incarnate. That being the case we can rely on what Jesus said about the Scriptures, and He said they cannot be broken. That gives us grounds to believe the Bible is authoritative.

The presuppositional approach starts with belief in the existence of God and the truth of Scripture. These serve as the foundation of the presuppositionalists' defense of the Christian faith. As long as they make valid implication and application of Scripture they will end up with the same basic beliefs as evidentialists. If there are differences, both will look to Scripture as the final court of appeal that will justify their belief. I have always sided with the evidentialists because it seems that if there is a dispute, one ends up citing evidence. For example, if the Mormon theologian said that one must start with belief in God and the truth of the Book of Mormon, most Christian theologians would counter that the Book of Mormon lacks evidence that the places it mentions ever existed or that its events ever happened. As a result, their presupposition must be rejected.

In 1984, R. C. Sproul, John Gerstner, and Arthur Lindsley published a book that defends the classical approach to apologetics which is grounded on rational evidence for the Christian faith.[196] They defend epistemological foundationalism and identify three "non-negotiable assumptions": the validity of the law of noncontradiction, the validity of the law of causality, and the basic reliability of sense perception.[197] The law of noncontradiction is stated simply as follows: "A cannot be A and non-A at the same time and in the same relationship."[198] Noncontradiction is a fascinating subject. During my seminary years I wrote a paper defending noncontradiction as being properly basic to foundational epistemology.[199] I concluded

195 Frank Morison, *Who Moved the Stone* (Grand Rapids: Zondervan, reprint of the 1930 edition).

196 R. C. Sproul, John Gerstner, Arthur Lindsley, *Classical Apologetics – A Rational Defense of the Christian Faith and a Critique of Presuppositional Apologetics* (Grand Rapids: Zondervan, Academie Books, 1984).

197 Ibid. 72.

198 Ibid.

199 http://cicministry.org/scholarly/sch004.htm

that since it is impossible to refute noncontradiction without using it, noncontradiction serves as a given of human rationality. Without it we would be unable to describe categories.

In an interesting turn in my debate with Doug Pagitt, I brought up noncontradiction as necessary for human rationality and communication. To my amazement he decided to debate the point by claiming that noncontradiction does not apply at the subatomic level. My response was that when I studied physical chemistry at Iowa State University we had to write complex formulas that involved predicting where electrons would be in their orbit (this is what quantum mechanics is about). All formulas depend on noncontradiction or they would be impossible to solve. I think what actually is the case is not that noncontradiction fails to apply to some aspects of reality, but that we do not understand some aspects of reality well enough to make adequate descriptions.[200]

The Emergent's purported reason for rejecting foundationalism is that the Enlightenment quest for knowledge based on scientific inquiry failed to produce total certainty about all things knowable in the real world. For example, Stanley Grenz and John R. Franke state "The goal of the foundationalist agenda is the discovery of an approach to knowledge that will provide rational human beings with absolute, incontestable certainty about the truthfulness of their beliefs."[201] This is a straw man argument because any approach to epistemology (foundationalist or otherwise) recognizes there are degrees of certainty, and foundationalists do not assert that finite man has "absolute, incontestable certainty" of knowledge.

I will let the second non-negotiable assumption, causality, stand on its own. But the third foundation, the basic reliability of sense perception, is under attack as well: "And with this concern [to find a sure foundation], the Enlightenment project assumed a realist metaphysic and evidenced a strong preference for the correspondence theory of truth, that is, the epistemological outlook that focuses on

200 Some skeptics and New Agers claim that subatomic physics invalidates noncontradiction because certain subatomic particles both exist and do not exist (which is meaningless) or come into existence from nonexistence. Whatever the case this is speculative and, more likely, is designed to attack the Biblical worldview than to further our understanding of the nature of the world.

201 Grenz, *Beyond,* 23.

the truth value of individual propositions and declares a proposition to be 'true' if and only if—or to the extent that—it corresponds with some fact."[202] Correspondence requires that humans test truth claims against the real world with their senses and God-given rational ability to interpret what they perceive in that world. This is not some dreamy speculative "theory," it is what humans must do every day to survive. For example, we must accurately perceive the difference between what is edible and inedible.

Let us step out of the world of philosophical speculation for a moment and into the real world. The postmodern theologians want us to believe that we cannot distinguish valid categories (non-contradiction), we cannot know cause and effect (causality), and we cannot test truth claims about things in the real world (reliability of sense perception). They claim that we live in a post-foundational world where most scholars acknowledge that the foundational approach has met its end because of the failure of the Enlightenment. But what they are really describing is the failure of rationalistic speculation that assumed man could understand everything in the universe without revelation from God. But in the real world of the hard sciences and engineering, the "modern" approach has not failed. We may not be able to describe all of reality with omniscience, but we do quite well in surviving in this world. For instance, who could claim that we know less about aeronautical engineering than we did in the 19th century?

The postmodern approach is a system of thought where people have raised the bar of human knowing to the level of divine-like omniscience, judged human knowing to be deficient by that standard, and on that basis rejected the whole project. What remains is "The Little Engine That Couldn't" in the real world while a system of knowledge is proffered out of the thin air of human consciousness. Postmoderns reject the foundation of Scripture on the grounds that its meaning is inaccessible, and they reject the foundation of evidence on the grounds that foundational approaches to knowledge died with the Enlightenment. The removal of foundations leaves us disconnected from the real world God created and the world of salvation history where God spoke, while putting us in a socially constructed world of a religious community.

---

202 Ibid. 32.

In the socially constructed world it is not possible to compare one religious community with another to determine whose beliefs are more "true." Even asking such a question was considered inappropriate as I found out when I asked Pagitt about it in our debate. (Remember that I had asked him if a Mormon Emerging Church would be valid. By postmodern standards, of course it would have to be—but Pagitt chose not to answer on the grounds that it was a "hypothetical" question.)

COHERENTISM

In order to avoid utter chaos in developing a theory of knowledge, postmoderns had to find a replacement for "failed" foundationalism. They call their answer "coherentism." Grenz and Franke describe it as follows: "At the heart of coherentism is the suggestion that the justification for a belief lies in its 'fit' with other held beliefs; hence, justification entails 'inclusion within a coherent system.'"[203] This system must not only be coherent, it also must have a means of interconnecting all of the parts in a "web of belief." Ironically, Grenz and Franke assert noncontradiction: "But what does it mean for a belief to cohere with other beliefs? Of course, noncontradiction must be an aspect of any coherence of beliefs."[204] But does not this make noncontradiction foundational and the very thing they wish to avoid? Furthermore, they state, ". . . the set of beliefs must form an integrated whole, and this whole must carry 'explanatory power.'"[205] But how can one test for "explanatory power" without some way to determine what does or does not correspond to the real world? If we have such a means, such as causality and sense perception, then we are back to foundationalism.

I have another nagging question about coherentism. Since the principle of coherence is taken for granted (i.e., a coherent system is valid but not an incoherent one), then is not coherence itself just another "foundation"? And if noncontradiction is necessary to test for coherence and coherence is accepted as necessary without any *a priori* reasoning, then apparently coherentism is another version of foundationalism with one important exception: it is disconnected

203 Ibid. 38.
204 Ibid. 39.
205 Ibid.

from the real world. How is that possible? Because it is possible to mentally construct a coherent system that is not internally contradictory that has no relationship to the universe we live in.

I once watched the film *Monsters, Inc.*[206] with my grandson. In the "world" of this animated film the city is powered by the screams of children. The monsters' job is to sneak into the kids' bedrooms at night and scare them as much as possible, thus keeping up the quota of needed power. The amazing thing about that movie is its coherence. As preposterous as its premise is, the movie coheres so well that everything in that fictional universe fits together seamlessly. The result is that it held my attention and created a desire to see what happens. Good works of fiction will do that.

But is coherent fiction adequate for a system of knowledge that unites a religious community? Do we not have to anchor our belief system in the real world? Perhaps we can construct a version that we prefer to the one we have experienced. To that end, Grenz and Franke cite Harold H. Joachim: "In our view it is the ideal which is solid and substantial and fully actual. The finite experiences are rooted in the ideal. They share its actuality, and draw from it whatever being and conceivability they possess."[207] Then Grenz and Franke comment on this, "Thus, the coherentist move away from foundationalism entailed a shift not only from the part to the whole, but also from the actual to the ideal."[208] It makes sense that if we are to have a mentally constructed reality that coheres, we should construct the most ideal version. But this differs little from romanticism–living in the mental world of our dreams rather than the actual tattered world around us.

Francis Schaeffer wrote about the deficiencies of romanticism:

> Christianity is not romantic; it is realistic. Christianity is realistic because it says that if there is no truth, there is also no hope; and there can be no truth if there is no adequate base. It is prepared to face the consequences of being proved false and say with Paul: If you find the

---

206 Monsters Inc. Co-Dir. Pete Docter and David Silverman. Pixar Animation Studios, 2001.

207 Harold J Joachim *The Nature of Truth* cited in Grenz *Beyond* 40.

208 Ibid. 40.

> body of Christ, the discussion is finished, let us eat and drink for tomorrow we die.[209]

Schaeffer was alluding to this passage: "*and if Christ has not been raised, your faith is worthless; you are still in your sins*" (**1Corinthians 15:17**). Biblical Christianity never claims that it should be believed because it gives the most romantically ideal view of the world. Its claims should be believed because Jesus Christ is the only one in history to predict His own resurrection from the dead on the third day, and actually rise and appear before many witnesses. His critics never claimed that His tomb was not empty.

The Bible is not romantically ideal and does not claim to be: It claims to be grounded in truth. Most people consider the message of the cross to be offensive or foolish (1Corinthians 1:23), and they are not naturally attracted to a message that states that most people are on the road to perdition, not salvation (Matthew 7:13, 14). Paul considered "worthless" any faith not grounded in the truth of what God did in Christ in real, tangible history.

Schaeffer saw the despair of his day because of the death of romanticism (which has now been given a rebirth in Emergent/postmodern religion) and even warned against "synthesis" which, as we saw in chapter 1, is precisely what is being embraced in the emergent movement:

> This [our seeming failure to give an answer in the face of despair] cannot be due to lack of opportunity; already men are part way to the Gospel, for they too believe that man is *dead*, dead in the sense of being meaningless, that their revolt has separated them from God who exists . . . But we cannot take advantage of our opportunity, *if we let go* in either thought or practice the methodology of antithesis. That is, that A is not non-A. If a thing is true, the opposite is not true; if a thing is right, the opposite is wrong. If our own young people within the churches and those of the world outside see us playing with the methodology

209 Francis Schaeffer, *The God Who is There* (Downers Grove: Intervarsity Press, 1968) 46.

> of synthesis . . . we can never expect to take advantage of this unique moment of opportunity presented by the death of romanticism.[210]

Schaeffer was amazingly prophetic. Romanticism did not stay dead; it has returned. The "synthesis" of which Schaeffer spoke was being introduced in Europe by Moltmann at about the same time Schaeffer wrote *The God Who is There*. The antithesis Schaeffer saw was this: either God is, has spoken, and has provided a means of salvation *or* life is meaningless as the nihilism of the mid-20th century asserted. Any synthesis would be false and fatal to Christianity in his estimation. The church failed to heed Schaeffer's dire warnings, and today an irrational synthesis has arrived.

In the idealism of postmodern coherentism, one is able to mentally escape the realities of the fallen world. Let me explain: If Moltmann and his modern followers are correct that God is in the future bringing the world into a better destiny, with our help, then God has always been in that state. So there should be some objective evidence of movement toward a paradise-like kingdom of God on earth. But in the 2,000 years since Christ's ascension we have seen only wars and human cruelty to continue worldwide. There is no objective evidence in history that the world is turning into the kingdom of God—and the Scripture teaches the opposite of it. At the end of history things will be much worse (Matthew 24:4-25; 2Timothy 3:1-13). In the real world, opposites do not synthesize into a better reality.

The opposites that exist create the backdrop for the hope of the gospel. Schaeffer made that quite clear:

> If we let go of our sense of antithesis, we will have nothing to say. Moreover, not only do we have nothing to say, we become nothing. Christianity ceases to exist, though it may still keep its outward institutional form. Christianity turns on antithesis, not as some abstract concept of truth, but in the fact that God exists, and in personal justification. The biblical concept of justification is a total, personal antithesis.

210 Ibid. 47.

> Before justification, we are dead in the kingdom of darkness. The Bible says that in the moment that we accept Christ we pass from death to life. This is total antithesis at the level of the individual man. Once we begin to slip over into the other methodology—a failure to hold on to an absolute which can be known by the whole man, including what is logical and rational in him—historic Christianity is destroyed.[211]

But in its exodus from all forms of foundationalism, rational or Biblical, postmodern theology has done exactly that—destroyed Christianity because there is no more antithesis. We are left with a mentally or socially constructed reality that may express some ideal world that does not really exist, but it cannot save us from the world of sin and darkness we really live in.

LIVING IN THE REAL WORLD

I have a very serious question to ask: what is more important, our eternal souls or the mundane things of ordinary life? Most would answer, "Our eternal souls, if they exist." Then my second question is this: why are we willing to accept a system of knowledge for our minds and souls that we would never accept for the mundane things of ordinary life?

Let me illustrate what I mean. Suppose two groups of people who knew nothing about mushrooms decided to go hunting for edible mushrooms growing in the forest. One group consists of foundationalists who believe in noncontradiction, causality, the reliability of sense knowledge and the correspondence theory of truth. The other group consists of postmodern coherentists who believe in socially constructed reality, group consensus, and reject the correspondence theory of truth, rational evidence, and scientific methodology.

Before the mushroom excursion, the first group hires an experienced mushroom expert to speak to the group. He demonstrates the characteristics of edible mushrooms using the best educational technology. The group is given all the objective tools necessary to distinguish the characteristics that separate non-edible mushrooms

---

211 Ibid.

from poisonous ones. They are given samples of edible mushrooms to observe with their physical senses.

Meanwhile, the postmodern group gets together for group meditation. Then they share their feelings about the woods, mushrooms, and the connectivity between all things. They imagine an ideal world where everything is in cooperation and humans dwell in perfect harmony with everything in nature and with one another. Once they feel this interconnectedness, they go forth to experience the finding and eating of mushrooms.

How many people would volunteer to be in the second group rather than the first? The danger of getting very sick or even dying by eating a poisonous mushroom is too great to risk doing it based on the subjectivity of a group experience. The irony, then, is that so many who would never risk their health and lives to such a process believe it makes perfect sense to do so with their eternal souls. So they accept the validity of foundationalism *in practice* when necessary for health in this life but reject it when it comes to *eternity*.

When I first read a book by an Emergent writer, I came to the conclusion that the best rebuttal to this thinking had been written years ago by Francis Schaeffer. Having since done much more extensive research I remain convinced of it. The rejection of a foundationalist epistemology has created an approach to religious truth that is disconnected from the real world. As such it is subject to having its religious claims autonomously exist in Schaeffer's famous "upper storey." Schaeffer warned about what would happen when pages were ripped from the Bible, leaving a partial book: "The parts of the pages which are discovered [which had been ripped out] correspond to the Scriptures which are God's propositional communication to mankind, which not only touch 'religious' truth but also touch the cosmos and history which are open to verification."[212] People have debated whether Schaeffer was a presuppositionalist or an evidentialist in his apologetics. Frankly, Schaeffer seemed presuppositionalist in his famous claim that religions and philosophies that cannot be lived and do not fit what we see in the world should be thereby rejected. But he defended the law of noncontradiction and believed that religious

212 Ibid. 108.

truth claims were open to verification. So we see evidence of both views. But as I have said, both are foundationalist.

But Schaeffer defended almost everything that Emergent/postmodern thinkers now attack, including propositional truth: "With the propositional communication from the personal God before us, not only the things of the cosmos and history match up but everything in the upper and lower storeys matches too; grace and nature; a moral absolute and morals; the universal point of reference and the particulars, and the emotional and aesthetic realities of man as well."[213] But this great benefit that Schaeffer describes is not available to those who reject foundationalism. First, those who reject foundationalism attack and reject the idea of "propositional communication" from God (i.e., they claim that the Bible cannot be a foundation for Christian theology). Then they question what we can know objectively about the world we live in on the grounds that our ability to perceive is not trustworthy. So they must construct a coherent mental world with a tenuous relationship at best to both the Scriptures and world (or to state it another way, despising both specific and general revelation). Schaeffer's upper and lower storeys not only fail to match in such a system; but even worse, both are emptied of objective content. Ironically, having made coherence the key test of truth, they have rejected the only true means of finding coherence.

But they call this a "theology of hope." In my opinion, the only reason such a hopeless approach to knowledge is labeled "hope" is the romantic notion that the world is going to turn into the kingdom of God without God bringing judgment at the end of history. That and the inconsistency of denying the validity of propositional truth that accurately corresponds to the real world all the while going about most of life using such knowledge and usually succeeding quite well at it. We do not need exhaustive knowledge like God's in order to live in the world He created. From the Scriptures we know enough about spiritual realities and of God Himself to find salvation if we believe the truth of the gospel and have assurance about future reward. Through studying general revelation we know enough about the created order to survive on the earth and enjoy God's good creation. We do not need to jettison this knowledge just because it is

213 Ibid. 109.

partial. And we will not gain paradise by rejecting this knowledge on the grounds that it reminds us that the world is not such a great place and will not get better until after cataclysmic judgment.

ACCOUNTABILITY TO GOD

Regarding theories of knowledge, postmodern theology consistently fails to address one topic: future judgment. This void characterizes nearly all Emergent/postmodern literature. The theology books that are more sophisticated than some, such as those of Grenz, Franke and Shults, do not contain any entry in their indexes under "judgment." Some Emergent books written on a more popular level either ignore or mock the entire matter of future judgment. Their authors especially do not want to see the cross as a substitutionary atonement in which God punishes His Son for the sins of believers. For example, British Emergent author Steve Chalke wrote, "If the cross is a personal act of violence perpetrated by God towards humankind but borne by his Son, then it makes a mockery of Jesus' own teaching to love your enemies and to refuse to repay evil with evil."[214] Be that as it may, they decry, avoid, or fail to address judgment.

I heard a podcast interview called "Bleeding Purple" in which Brian McLaren called the doctrine of hell, "Bad advertising for God." Here is part of the transcript:

> But that the kingdom of God comes through suffering and willing, voluntary sacrifice. But in an ironic way, the doctrine of hell basically says, no, that that's not really true. That in the end, God gets His way through coercion and violence and intimidation and domination, just like every other kingdom does. The cross isn't the center then. The cross is almost a distraction and false advertising for God.[215]

214 Steve Chalke, *The Lost Message of Jesus*, (Grand Rapids: Zondervan, 2003) 182 - 183 cited from D. A. Carson, *Becoming Conversant With The Emerging Church* (Grand Rapids: Zondervan, 2005) 185.

215 The transcript is posted here: http://www.understandthetimes.org/mclarentrans.shtml (accessed 1/10/08).

McLaren also recounts how he used to believe the evangelical theology of, "Christ being a substitutionary sacrifice for my sin," but now views that idea to be "Paulianity" not Christianity.[216] He sees Jesus' teaching that the kingdom is at hand to be antithetical to this idea: "Paulianity is about a select few escaping earth and going to heaven after they die."[217] Later we shall deal with the issue of defining the kingdom, but for now we are seeing that the possibility of future judgment and punishment of those who do not believe in Christ's death on the cross and His shedding of blood to avert God's wrath against sin is either denied or not discussed in Emergent/postmodern theology. This issue is very important to our understanding of knowledge.

If there is a literal future judgment (in spite of the fact that some prefer a universe without one), the question becomes whether or not we know enough to be accountable to God on that day. At a debate I witnessed between a Christian and a famous secular humanist, the Christian said, "but if there really is a God, what will you do on the Day of Judgment"? The humanist answered, "I will tell him that he cannot judge me because he failed to provide enough evidence for me to believe." But, of course, the humanist does not believe the Bible. And the Bible states quite the opposite: "*For the wrath of God is revealed from heaven against all ungodliness and unrighteousness of men who suppress the truth in unrighteousness, because that which is known about God is evident within them; for God made it evident to them*" (**Romans 1:18, 19**). If the Scriptures are God-breathed as indeed they claim to be (2Timothy 3:16), those who respond like the humanist are in serious trouble. God has provided what we need in order to be accountable.

What Paul asserted is that to merely be observant of the creation (general revelation) is sufficient to make humans accountable to God. What is more, in his litany of human sinfulness spanning Romans 1:18 to Romans 3:20, Paul asserts that all humans have sinned against every form of knowledge that they have had. The Gentiles sin against general revelation (as just cited) and against their own consciences (Romans 2:14 - 16) as well. The Jews, who have specific revelation, have sinned against the Law (Romans 2:17-24). The sorry

216 Brian McLaren, *The Secret Message of Jesus – Uncovering the Truth That Could Change Everything* (Nashville: W Publishing Group, 2006) 91.
217 Ibid.

reality is that man has rejected every means God has used to communicate His truth to him. The future is bleak for those who do not turn to God through the gospel: "*But because of your stubbornness and unrepentant heart you are storing up wrath for yourself in the day of wrath and revelation of the righteous judgment of God, who will render to each person according to his deeds*" (**Romans 2:5, 6**). Accountability to God is forthrightly asserted to be true.

A mentally or socially constructed world that we might consider coherent and favorable to our own view of things will not save us on the Day of Judgment or reveal God's plan of salvation. Such an imagined world will not change the certainty of future judgment or remove accountability on the grounds that we lack knowledge: "*Now we know that whatever the Law says, it speaks to those who are under the Law, so that every mouth may be closed and all the world may become accountable to God*" (**Romans 3:19**) In the Greek Paul said those who are "in the law." Does he mean only Jews who had the Law? The context says otherwise, since this passage is at the end of his long litany about universal sin against every form of self-revelation God has given. I agree with Murray who concludes:

> This [that Paul uses universal terminology and included the Gentiles as accountable in chapter 2] establishes the all-important consideration that although the Gentiles did not have the Old Testament law and in that sense were without law, yet they were not outside the sphere of the judgment which the Old Testament pronounced. This is saying that the descriptions given in those passages quoted [Romans 3:10 - 18] were characteristic of the Gentiles as well as of the Jews and the corresponding judgment rested upon them to the end that they might all be without excuse and be condemned in the sight of God.[218]

The truth is that the Bible states that a future judgment will be held and that everyone will be accountable to God.

---

218 John Murray, "The Epistle to the Romans," in *The New International Commentary on the New Testament* (Grand Rapids: Eerdmans, 1965) 106, 107.

Paul teaches universal sinfulness and accountability to highlight the need for the gospel and the glorious nature of salvation. He teaches expressly what McLaren and many other Emergent/postmodern teachers refuse to believe–that God provided a substitutionary atonement to satisfy His own demands for justice *and to* save those who believe:

> *But now apart from the Law the righteousness of God has been manifested, being witnessed by the Law and the Prophets, even the righteousness of God through faith in Jesus Christ for all those who believe; for there is no distinction; for all have sinned and fall short of the glory of God, being justified as a gift by His grace through the redemption which is in Christ Jesus; whom God displayed publicly as a propitiation in His blood through faith. This was to demonstrate His righteousness, because in the forbearance of God He passed over the sins previously committed; for the demonstration, I say, of His righteousness at the present time, so that He would be just and the justifier of the one who has faith in Jesus.* (**Romans 3:21 – 26**)

Paul's term translated "propitiation" (which means "appeasing God's wrath against sin") is used in Hebrews 9:5 in reference to the "mercy seat" that covered the Ark of the Covenant in the Old Testament. On the Day of Atonement the high priest poured out the blood of the sacrifice upon it. Whether Chalke and McLaren think this idea is incompatible with God's loving character or not, Paul obviously taught it. He also told us the reason it was necessary that Christ's blood would be the price of redemption–so that God would be "just and the justifier" of believers.

Chalke says that, if true, this would be "cosmic child-abuse": "The fact is that the cross isn't a form of cosmic child abuse–a vengeful Father, punishing his Son for an offense he has not even committed."[219] But Paul expressly said that Christ's shed blood demonstrated God's righteousness in passing over sins. McLaren, after his comments on "Paulianity," goes on to cite selected passages from Paul that McLaren claims can be seen as supportive of McLaren's idea

219 Chalk, *Lost Message* as cited in Carson *Conversant*, 185.

of the kingdom. But this selectivity makes no attempt to understand Paul's message in its entirety.

In critiquing someone's message, it is only right to assume they have cogent ideas and that those ideas are coherent if they are a good writer. I have made that assumption about McLaren in my attempt to understand him, but I have no time for straw man arguments. It is only satisfying to debate what someone actually believes, not a caricature that is easier to refute. That is why I did not begin writing this book until after I went to great lengths to find out what Emergent/postmodern authors believe and where those beliefs came from. The task was not easy since the Emergent/postmodern authors are rather coy about their beliefs. Nor was it easy to read Moltmann—but I did so as soon as I discovered the influence he wielded. We must be honest and fair.

If it is right and necessary to approach contemporary authors that way, should we not be required to do the same with Biblical authors? McLaren must not agree because he does not extend the same courtesy to Paul. One cannot dismiss Paul's express teachings on atonement as "Paulianity" only later to cite him elsewhere in support of a version of the social gospel. If one desires to read Paul responsibly, he must assume that Paul himself is a coherent writer and is not contradicting himself (even if he falsely dismisses the idea of the inspiration of Scripture). The same can be said for John, who also taught about God's wrath: "*He who believes in the Son has eternal life; but he who does not obey the Son will not see life, but the wrath of God abides on him.*" (**John 3:36**). The gospel writers must be studied in their entirety.

No matter the epistemology people adhere to, they must first understand what the Biblical authors meant if they choose to cite the Bible in defense of their theology (even if they reject the traditional evangelical view of Scripture as being inspired, authoritative and inerrant). We cannot understand any author's meaning without a hermeneutic that makes knowing such meaning possible. Furthermore, we cannot know what an author means if we fail to consider their body of written work. We cannot select some of the "red letters" and massage them in order to teach the social gospel and then reject the others that don't support our hypothesis.

Paul made it clear that he considered everyone accountable, that there is such a thing as God's wrath against sin, that Jesus died to satisfy that wrath, and that faith in Christ is necessary for anyone to be justified before God. That is not hard to understand from reading Romans. We could dare to claim that Paul was dead wrong, but we cannot claim he did not teach it.

FOUNDATIONALISM IS INESCAPABLE

The foundationalism that Emergent/postmodern writers disparage was not invented by the Enlightenment; it is merely descriptive of humans bearing God's image. We need noncontradiction in order to describe categories. It is seen in the Garden of Eden: Eating of the tree of the knowledge of good and evil is not the same as not eating of the tree at the same time and in the same relationship. Nor do eating and not eating synthesize into a third and better alternative. Sproul and co-writers point this out: "The Bible describes the fall of the human race in terms of a trial hanging on a contradiction."[220]

Likewise, we cannot escape causality. Every effect must have a cause. We could not function as rational creatures if this were not true. Again citing Sproul, "Like the law of noncontradiction, it is something which all in fact believe because all *must* believe it in order to function as human beings."[221] If a person went to work with his house intact and came home to find a pile of ashes, but did not believe in causality, he would have to scratch his head and ponder the idea of what once was wood and now is ashes with no way to understand how such a change could exist. If one did not believe that putting his hand in a fire *caused* the resultant pain, he would have no reason to refrain from putting his hand into the fire again. Attacks against foundationalism are merely attacks against humans being created in God's image. We may not *understand* every cause in a complex world, but we cannot deny the necessity that there are always causes for events.

Though we must admit that as fallen humans our sense perception is limited and fraught with problems, we cannot deny the basic reliability of the physical senses without denying our very beings as human. Sproul and co-authors explain:

220 Sproul, *Classical*, 81.
221 Ibid. 83.

> Our senses are limited but not impotent; they are problematic, but not useless. But with all these qualifiers, how can we be sure that our senses are even basically reliable and not totally distortive? We cannot. That is why we are left with the common sense necessity of assuming it. The reliability of sense perception must be a working presupposition if knowledge of the external world is to be possible.[222]

That is why sense perception is foundational. It is an inescapable reality of being humans in God's image. We can claim that we have no access whatsoever to the world God created and put us in, but we cannot live that way. We must have a means of perceiving that world to live in it. People who have lost their sense perception, such as being in a deep coma, must be cared for by people who have retained their sense perception.

As we have shown, Paul makes our sense perception (Romans 1:20) foundational for human accountability before God. But there is something greater than sense perception of the created universe; there is God's self-revelation to us in words that He chose (Hebrews 1:1, 2). God provided evidence in history that these are His words by sending the Incarnate Word who spoke, who offered his own death, burial, and resurrection as proof of His divine identity, and appeared to witnesses who were charged to testify that He indeed had rose from the dead.

To reject both forms of Christian foundationalism, that which begins with evidence for the veracity of Scripture and that which begins with Scripture itself, is to create a religion detached from the world where God has acted and spoken. Such a religion is constructed in a world of ideas that needs bear no connection to the observable world. But we cannot truly *escape from reason* (to use Schaeffer's term). Here is what he wrote in a book by the same title:

> The Bible does not set out unrelated thoughts. The system it sets forth has a beginning and moves from that beginning in a non-contradictory way. The

222 Ibid. 87.

> beginning is the existence of the infinite-personal God as Creator of all else. Christianity is not just a vague set of incommunicable experiences, based on a totally unverifiable 'leap in the dark'.[223]

Schaeffer claimed that the problem with the Enlightenment project was not rationality, but the positing of a closed system in which God cannot act or speak. But God is there and has spoken. The rejection of foundationalism is a rejection of rationality which is a rejection of the God who has spoken. And as we have claimed, it is a rejection of human accountability to God in future judgment. But accountability does not vanish with people's epistemological musings.

In the next chapter we shall explore the Biblical teaching about the kingdom of God and compare it to what Emergent/post-modern writers have to say about it.

223 Francis A. Schaeffer, *Escape from Reason* (Downers Grove, Intervarsity Press, 1968) 91.

Abstract Chapter 8

Undefining the Kingdom of God

KINGDOM OF GOD = JOINING GOD AND BUILDING AN EARTHLY PARADISE NOW

Emergent's "kingdom of God" is the logical result of their eschatology—all things are coming together in a future paradise. In scripture when the "King" of God comes, we see a threat to all who do not obey the King's laws or commands. There are no lawbreakers or evildoers in the kingdom of God when the King returns; they are all punished and judged. For non-citizens, the kingdom of God is judgment. The coming of the kingdom of God is judgment and retribution to its enemies; reward and blessing comes only to those who are already citizens. The only way to become a citizen is to believe in Christ's substitutionary death on the cross for one's sins. "The blessed hope" of Christ's return to take the throne of His kingdom only is for those who have trusted Him for salvation.

REPACKAGED SOCIAL GOSPEL + MYSTICAL SPIRITUALITY

The kingdom of God as defined by the Emergent is simply a repackaged social gospel, one in which all people must find a way to make this world a better place while waiting for it to be perfected as they move toward a future paradise. For the Emergent, all that really matters is that we discover a problem to care about and do our best to correct it. Emergents call this, "joining the kingdom of God wherever we may find it." For all their claims, this social gospel is nothing new or groundbreaking—it is just repackaged liberalism. The trouble with this approach is that "fixing social problems" doesn't address the most crucial aspect of "joining the kingdom of God." That crucial aspect, the one that the Son of God died for, is that lawbreakers be reconciled to God through Jesus Christ and become citizens. Until we are citizens we are not part of the kingdom of God. Lawbreakers doing good deeds are still lawbreakers outside the kingdom. They have not become citizens according to the King's terms and have no future to look forward to when the King arrives–except judgment. Helping God create a future utopia is the opposite of the kingdom of God in scripture. The Emergent have taken the Christian term "kingdom of God" and perverted its meaning in order to fit their eschatology.

8

Undefining the Kingdom of God

A key characteristic of Emergent/postmodern theology is how they view the kingdom of God—how they teach the concept. In our debate, Doug Pagitt's first point in his opening remarks was this: [We are] "Kingdom of God focused and we want to join the kingdom of God wherever we find it." They consider the kingdom to be something found through human inquiry and then joined. Many other Emergent statements claim that the kingdom is emerging now, in world history, through processes that we can get involved with.

In this chapter we will see that Emergent writers' the use of the term "kingdom of God" is not based on any biblical definition, but on vague ideas about how to make the world a better place to live in.

A KINGDOM THAT IS OF THIS WORLD

In chapter 2 we saw that Brian McLaren obscured what John's gospel says about the kingdom. There Jesus said, "My kingdom is not of this world." In *The Secret Message of Jesus*, McLaren spends several chapters writing about that kingdom. Reading those chapters is frustrating because he offers no clear definition of what the kingdom of God is. But since the message of the kingdom is "secret" according to McLaren, it follows that his version of it is not clearly defined. He writes, "[D] epending on how we respond to his secret message of the kingdom of God, we will create two very different worlds, two very difference futures–one hellish, the other heavenly."[224] But note: he is speaking of earthly realities, not differing eternal future destinies.

He confuses his readers by the use of the term "secret." The meaning of the term "kingdom of God" either is revealed or unrevealed. If revealed it is not "secret" (see Deuteronomy 29:29 to learn how that term is used in the Bible). If revealed by the Holy Spirit-inspired Scriptures a doctrine of the kingdom can be gleaned and expressed through valid Biblical exegesis that deals with pertinent passages. But that is not McLaren's procedure. Consider his use of the phrase "weeping and gnashing":

> One world is all too familiar to us. It is a future too much like our past: full of regret and pain–which is exactly what hellish language like "weeping and gnashing of teeth" is intended to evoke. It is a world of increasing violence and disease, environmental degradation and economic disaster, division at every level of society, and on an individual level–fear, guilt, anxiety, lust, greed, pain.[225]

McLaren gives no exegetical evidence that "weeping and gnashing of teeth" when used in connection with the kingdom of God means "bad outcomes throughout history."

When we consult the Bible on this matter we find that its meaning is not cryptic, but clear:

> *Again, the kingdom of heaven is like a dragnet cast into the sea, and gathering fish of every kind; and when it was filled, they drew it up on the beach; and they sat down, and gathered the good fish into containers, but the bad they threw away. So it will be at the end of the age; the angels shall come forth, and take out the wicked from among the righteous, and will*

---

224 Brian McLaren, *The Secret Message of Jesus – Uncovering the Truth That Could Change Everything*, (Nashville: W Publishing Group, 2006); 181.

225 Ibid.

> *cast them into the furnace of fire; there shall be weeping and gnashing of teeth.* (**Matthew 13:47-50**)

Jesus explicitly said that this happens at the end of the age, not throughout the process of history. He spoke not of societal problems such as violence and pollution but of the final judgment. The two types of fish in the net are a simile for two types of people and their differing fates at the end of the age. The verse is about literal future judgment, not unhappy consequences in history.

Furthermore, the context shows that this is thematic in Matthew: "*Therefore just as the tares are gathered up and burned with fire, so shall it be at the end of the age. The Son of Man will send forth His angels, and they will gather out of His kingdom all stumbling blocks, and those who commit lawlessness, and will cast them into the furnace of fire; in that place there shall be weeping and gnashing of teeth*" (**Matthew 13:40 – 42**). But because Emergent/postmodern theology rejects the idea of a literal future judgment, McLaren teases his readers with ideas linked to Scripture passages ("weeping and gnashing of teeth") and refuses to submit his ideas to the authority of Scripture. Jesus made it clear that this happens at the end of the age, and being thrown into a "furnace of fire" is not about unhappy social conditions in the here and now.

Rob Bell teaches the same idea that heaven and hell are choices about how life will be on earth now:

> Now if there is a life of heaven, and we can choose it, then there's also another way. A way of living out of sync with how God created us to live. [sic] The word for this is *hell*: a way, a place, a realm absent of how God desires things to be. We can bring heaven to earth; we can bring hell to earth. For Jesus, heaven and hell were present realities. Ways of living we can enter into here and now.[226]

Bell's idea of the kingdom is revealed in his understanding of the Lord's Prayer: "This is why Jesus taught his disciples to pray, 'May your will be done on earth as it is in heaven.' There is this place, this

226 Rob Bell, *Velvet Elvis – Rethinking the Christian Faith* (Zondervan: Grand Rapids, 2005) 147.

realm, heaven, where things are as God desires them to be. As we live this way, heaven comes here. To this place, this world, the one we're living in."[227] But the prayer for the "kingdom" to come is a prayer for the return of Christ who will literally reign on the earth–and that only after He brings judgment. In Emergent/postmodern theology there is no literal, future judgment, but only consequences now.

Pagitt's understanding of the Kingdom of God is much like McLaren's and Bell's:

> We aid the Spirit in the work of the Kingdom by making all things better in our own time and place. This understanding of the story entails that creativity is a central activity of the Kingdom of God. Imagine the Kingdom of God as the creative process of God reengaging in all that we know and experience. Imagine what it means to wonder if Jesus used so many metaphors for the Kingdom of God not because he couldn't find the right words, but because the Kingdom is like so many things, and so many things are like the Kingdom. When we employ creativity to make this world better, we participate with God in the re-creation of the world.[228]

In chapter 1 we reviewed Pagitt's idea of re-creation within the context of emergent eschatology. Here it serves to illustrate the tendency to divorce the idea of the kingdom of God from any serious, Biblical exegesis of the pertinent passages. Jesus' metaphors had definite meanings and those meanings are to be determined by a hermeneutic that seeks to understand the Biblical authors' intent. If Jesus wished to teach that humans have the power to re-create the world, to make it a better place, and that this creative process is how the kingdom is going to unfold He would have done so. But He did not. He did, however, warn that He would return at an unexpected time and bring judgment and did so in many teachings and many parables (see for example Matthew 24:36-25:46).

---

227 Ibid.

228 Doug Pagitt, *Church Re-imagined* (Grand Rapids: Zondervan, 2003/2005) 185.

SOCIALLY CONSTRUCTED "REALITY"

Stanley Grenz and John R. Franke have a similar idea but see the process of making a better world to be the function of language in a social community:

> As the community of Christ, we have a divinely given mandate: to be participants in God's work of constructing a world that reflects God's own will for creation, a world in which everything finds its connectedness in Jesus Christ (Col. 1:17) who is the *logos*, the ordering principal of the cosmos as God intends it to be. This mandate has a strongly linguistic dimension. We participate with God as we, through the constructive power of language, create a world that links our present with the divine future, or we should say, as the Holy Spirit creates such a world in, among, and through us.[229]

Time and again in Emergent/postmodern theology the idea appears that God needs our help in order to make the world into that of His dreams. But how could our communal words "create" a new world? God spoke, and the world came into existence and was good; it happened before there were humans around to help Him! The only "help" that humans gave was to rebel and plunge the world into sin and darkness. In a fit of postmodern optimism, these theologians assume that human works can undo the damage done by human rebellion.

They base their hope on the idea of a socially constructed "reality": "The simple fact is, we do not inhabit the 'world-in-itself'; instead, we live in a linguistic world of our own making. As Berger and Luckmann note, human reality is 'socially constructed reality.'"[230] They assume that if reality is socially "constructed" it can be socially "deconstructed" and socially "reconstructed" to a much better, ideal future "reality."

---

229 Stanley Grenz and John R. Franke, *Beyond Foundationalism – Shaping Theology in a Postmodern Context* (Louisville: Westminster John Knox Press, 2001). 53.

230 Ibid.

Let's accept their premise (false as it is) and consider one implication. All the Emergent/postmodern writers we have studied decry the world as it is, or else they would not promote re-creating it. If indeed the world we now live in was socially constructed as they claim, then the evil in it was socially constructed. This suggests that the process of socially constructing an evil world rather than a good one has gone on throughout human history by anyone's reading of history. Bernard Ramm discusses Edward O. Wilson's book (*Sociobiology*) on the horrible human condition: "In his book he observes that the human species (as far as its recorded history is concerned) is at war forty-eight percent of the time."[231] The "socially constructed" world we inhabit has been unabatedly sinful since the Fall.

This being the case, how does a community break free from this condition and "construct" a new social world? The "worlds" that have been created by sinners have always been evil sinful worlds. Grenz and Franke claim that the Holy Spirit working through a Christian community is going to change that. But the Holy Spirit was poured out on the Day of Pentecost, and He has been working in Christian communities for the last 2,000 years—and in not one of them has He yet re-created the world into the kingdom of God. Christians are forgiven and sanctified, but not perfected. Furthermore, in church history all of these groups—the State Church, post-millennialism, the social gospel, dominion theology, spiritual warfare theology, and the latter day apostles—have claimed to have the means to change the world into some version of the kingdom of God. None has. Did they all fail because they did not understand the "power of language" and "socially constructed reality"—or did they fail because sin is entrenched in humanity and this world will not become the kingdom of God until Christ returns to judge sin and remove all unrepentant sinners from His kingdom? The Bible says the latter.

Grenz and Franke do not solve this problem but push it into the future. They comment on how there can be "objectivity" even if the "world-in-itself" cannot be known:

---

231 Bernard Ramm, *Offense to Reason – The Theology of Sin* (New York: Harper and Row, 1985) 24.

> Rather, seen through the lense [sic] of the gospel, this objectivity is the objectivity of the world as God wills it to be. Because what God wills is not a present but a future reality (e.g. Isa. 65:17-19; Rev. 21:5), the "objectivity of the world" about which we can truly speak is an objectivity of a *future*, eschatological world. And because this future reality is God's determined will for creation, as that which cannot be shaken (Heb. 12:26-28) it is far more real–more objectively real–than the present world, which is even now passing away (1Cor. 7:31).

By referencing Hebrews 12:28 they are bringing in the idea of the kingdom of God. This does not prove "socially constructed reality" nor does it explain objectivity. A present "objectivity" of a future eschatological world is only meaningful if we believe the scriptures that explain the future world (as their citations of Scripture indicate). But what is objective to us now is not the future, but the Scriptures themselves. The only access we have to the future is the promise of God objectively understood by Scriptures whose meaning can be known. Furthermore, the reason to believe the Scriptures is the objectivity of the evidence that God acted in history and has spoken to us through His Son (Hebrews 1:1, 2). But as we saw in chapter 5, Grenz and Franke deny that there can be "objectivity of exegesis."

Consider what a tangled mess this version of postmodern theology leaves us: 1) We are stuck in a socially constructed "reality." 2) Our socially constructed world is full of evil and wickedness and has been since the Fall. 3) We can be optimistic because we can participate with God through the constructive power of language to make a new socially constructed world–with the help of the Holy Spirit. 4) All previous Christian communities with the Holy Spirit who have attempted to make this world into the kingdom of God have failed, but that fact should not affect our thinking. 5) We can be objective and hopeful about the future eschatological world because Scripture predicts that it will be a good one. 6) We cannot be objective in exegesis of Scripture so we cannot know what the Bible means in a non-relativistic way. 7) This is supposed to make sense and be hopeful? Calling this a theology of hope is indeed an attempt to alter reality by use of words, because outside of words we will find no rational hope in this system of beliefs. Unless, that is, God is indeed drawing everything into Himself with a huge "tractor beam of redemption" as we cited Tony Jones in chapter 1. But based on their own hermeneutic they cannot prove by Scripture we are on such a "tractor beam." Based on a literal hermeneutic we can show that Scripture teaches the world is headed toward judgment.

THE UNDEFINED WORD "KINGDOM"

Throughout this book I have made reference to the fact that in his day Francis Schaeffer identified and rejected theology and ideas that have now resurfaced in Emergent/postmodern theology. Schaeffer warned against what he called "semantic mysticism" which was a means of using words for their value in creating connotation while disconnecting them from rational meaning. In other words, allowing words to connote but not denote. He claimed that neo-orthodoxy purposely used words that had connotations that seemed more hopeful than the bleak outlook of secular existentialism but in fact had been stripped of their rational content. Schaeffer's discussion of semantic mysticism will help us understand how the Emergent/postmodern use of "kingdom of God" is an example of the type of semantic mysticism Schaeffer confronted in his day.

Schaeffer begins by explaining how words retain their connotation in people's minds even after their content has been removed:

> Every word has two parts. There is the dictionary definition and there is the connotation. Words may be synonymous by definition but have completely different connotations. Therefore we find that when a symbol as *the cross* is used, whether in writing or painting, a certain connotation stirs the mind of people brought up in a Christian culture, even if they have rejected Christianity. . . So when the new theology uses such words, without definition, an

> illusion of meaning is given which is pragmatically useful in arousing deep motivations.[232]

I have used the theme "undefining" throughout this book because I believe that what Schaeffer identifies is precisely what is happening in the Emergent Church. It is happening today for the very reason it happened in the 20th century: to give the allusion of hope to a system of theology that logically yields only despair. Here is Schaeffer's assessment: "The secret of the strength of neo-orthodoxy is that these religious symbols with a connotation of personality give an illusion of meaning, and as a consequence it appears to be more optimistic than secular existentialism."[233] Reading the works of many Emergent writers reveals that they consistently speak of hope and use terms found in Christianity such as the kingdom of God, but the terms remained undefined.

Likewise the symbol of the cross is found in services, such as a photo I saw of a young woman writing her name on a wooden cross. But in the Emergent Church the doctrine of the cross, which involves the substitutionary atonement, either is ignored or denied. (However, the symbol retains its connotative value.) The only reason the symbol in the photo was a cross, in my opinion, is that this was a church in America, where Christianity has been a prevalent religion. Writing one's name on a symbol of Buddhism, such as the eight-spoked Dharmacakra for most Americans would not have the same connotation as the cross. But an undefined cross says no more than an undefined Dharmacakra. One could have an Emergent Buddhist service in India with Buddhist symbols for people to write their names on, and they would have an experience similar to that of the Emergent American and her cross.

For many years the church of which I am a pastor met in a building in the inner city. Often, homeless men would set up cardboard shanties and sleep on our church's front steps. I asked one of them why he had set up "shop" on our front steps. His answer was that it made him feel closer to God. I told him that a church building is no closer to God than a park or a cemetery. The only way to get close to

232 Francis Schaeffer, *The God Who is There* (Downers Grove: Intervarsity Press, 1968) 57.

233 Ibid. 58.

God, I said, was through the gospel of Jesus Christ, which I proceeded to share with him. He was not interested in the gospel; the front steps of the church were as close to God as he wanted to be. Similarly, many think Christian words or symbols make them feel closer to God. (But they do not want the content of the gospel preached to them because it offends them.) In like fashion, the Emergent Church is offering a way to *feel* like one is participating in the kingdom of God without offering the only terms of entrance to the kingdom—which is to repent and believe the gospel.

I believe that the term "kingdom of God" is used so regularly in Emergent literature because in many people's minds it has no clearly defined meaning. It is not the easiest concept in the Bible to understand (which makes it subject to uses that depart from the Biblical definition.) Schaeffer discusses how, in semantic mysticism, obscurity is useful: "*To the new theology, the usefulness of a symbol is in direct proportion to its obscurity.* There is connotation, as in the word *god*, but there is no definition."[234] The semantic mysticism that Schaeffer identified, even down to how "God" is discussed characterizes Emergent/postmodern theology. For example, McLaren writes about his generous orthodoxy: "It doesn't consider orthodoxy the exclusive domain of prose scholars (theologians) alone but, like Chesterton, welcomes the poets, the mystics, and even those who choose to say very little or remain silent, including the disillusioned and the doubters. Their silence speaks eloquently of the majesty of God that goes beyond all human articulation."[235] Statements like this are direct examples of what Schaeffer called "semantic mysticism." Nothing is being communicated. Schaeffer gave a similar example from existential theologian Paul Tillich's phrase, "God behind God."[236]

Let us return to Pagitt's point in the debate, "to join the kingdom of God wherever we find it." What does that statement describe? What separates kingdom from non-kingdom? He does not define the "kingdom," so there is no way to know what to look for. By all accounts, Emergent practitioners look for social action happening and see the kingdom there. The *Secret Message of Jesus* is an articulation of the social gospel, and McLaren's heroes who have paid a price for the

234 Ibid. Italics in original.

235 Brian D. McLaren, *a Generous Orthodoxy* (El Cajon, CA: Youth Specialties, 2004; published by Zondervan) 155.

236 Schaeffer, 58.

"kingdom" are Martin Luther King Jr., Bishop Romero, Desmond Tutu, and Nelson Mandela.[237] An essay writer in *Emergent Manifesto of Hope* expresses her idea of the kingdom this way:

> We are recognizing our responsibility to strive to bring holistic freedom and salvation to all humankind. We dare to think new thoughts and dream new dreams. We choose to extend God's kingdom into new areas, not being content to limit our role to the narrowest conceivable definition of "spirituality."[238]

It is praiseworthy that people do good deeds to help the impoverished and oppressed. But does the presence of social action mean the presence of God's kingdom? Many world religions promote good works as part of their belief system. Does one find the "kingdom" when one sees someone doing a good work in the name of a false god? I think not.

Furthermore, the semantic mysticism expressed by these authors allows people to use their own imagination to fill the void left because of the lack of definition. One could reasonably argue that the only reason people like McLaren see social action as the "kingdom" is because of their own personal prejudices and inclinations. Someone who embraces the health and wealth gospel could claim to find the kingdom through building a profitable business (they do, in fact, claim this—building "for the kingdom"). To "find" the kingdom and join it with the term "kingdom" undefined is to find activities or people with certain ideas that one may resonate with, and then get involved. But this has nothing to do with the Biblically defined kingdom of God.

THE BIBLICALLY DEFINED KINGDOM OF GOD

To define the kingdom of God one first must determine the identity of God's "king." The promise of a future kingdom was given to David in the Old Testament:

237 McLaren, *Message*, 169.

238 Deborah and Ken Loyd, "Our Report Card in the Year 2057 – A Reflection on Women's Rights, Poverty, and Oppression" in *An Emergent Manifesto of Hope* Doug Pagitt and Tony Jones editors (Grand Rapids: Baker, 2007) 276.

> *When your days are complete and you lie down with your fathers, I will raise up your descendant after you, who will come forth from you, and I will establish his kingdom. He shall build a house for My name, and I will establish the throne of his kingdom forever. I will be a father to him and he will be a son to Me; when he commits iniquity, I will correct him with the rod of men and the strokes of the sons of men, but My lovingkindness shall not depart from him, as I took it away from Saul, whom I removed from before you. And your house and your kingdom shall endure before Me forever; your throne shall be established forever.* (**2Samuel 7:12–16**)

It is important to understand Bible prophecy in such a way that we do not misinterpret it. Prophecy often combines ideas such as the near and the far, the many and the one, and the already and the not yet. Such is the case with the Messianic prophecy just cited. Some of it applies to Solomon (who commits iniquity, builds a house), and other aspects of it apply to Messiah (the throne of His kingdom forever). We do not have to rely solely on this hermeneutical principle because, in this case, David explicitly said that he understood it that way: "*And yet this* [God's previous work in David's life] *was insignificant in Thine eyes, O Lord God, for Thou hast spoken also of the house of Thy servant concerning the distant future. And this is the custom of man, O Lord God*" (**2Samuel 7:19**). To further show this principle, Hebrews 1:5 cites only the Messianic part, "I will be a Father to Him and He will be a Son to Me," and applies it to Christ.

The New Testament claims that Jesus Christ is the promised Davidic king. For example, Matthew begins his gospel calling Jesus "the son of David" and gives us a genealogy to prove it. Any study of the kingdom of God must begin with the Biblical claim that Jesus is indeed the promised King. This claim caused Jesus to be mocked on the cross: "*He saved others; He cannot save Himself. He is the King of Israel; let Him now come down from the cross, and we shall believe in Him*" (**Matthew 27:42**). The fact that Jesus claimed to be the Davidic king (Matthew 27:11) and that He was subsequently crucified sparked the debate between Christians and Jews that carries on to this day. How could the person who was to sit on the throne of David die the death of a condemned criminal, and in such a cursed manner as hanging on a tree (Deuteronomy 21:33 and Galatians 3:13)?

One of the interesting documents of early church history is Justin Martyr's *Dialogue with Trypho a Jew.* (The debate took place in 135 A.D. but was written down later by Justin.) One of the key points of contention was Trypho's claim that a crucified man was cursed according to the Law, so he could not be the Messiah. Here is part of Justin's rebuttal of that idea:

> For tell me, was it not God who commanded by Moses that no image or likeness of anything which was in heaven above or which was on the earth should be made, and yet who caused the brazen serpent to be made by Moses in the wilderness, and set it up for a sign by which those bitten by serpents were saved? Yet is He free from unrighteousness. For by this, as I previously remarked, He proclaimed the mystery, by which He declared that He would break the power of the serpent which occasioned the transgression of Adam, and [would bring] to them that believe on Him [who was foreshadowed] by this sign, i.e., Him who was to be crucified, salvation from the fangs of the serpent, which are wicked deeds, idolatries, and other unrighteous acts. Unless the matter be so understood, give me a reason why Moses set up the brazen serpent for a sign, and bade those that were bitten gaze at it, and the wounded were healed; and this, too, when he had himself commanded that no likeness of anything whatsoever should be made.[239]

To that Trypho admitted his Jewish teachers could not answer why God commanded Moses to make a brazen serpent (which was unlawful according to Moses' own teachings), and that people were healed simply by looking upon it. That gave Justin the opportunity to point

239 Roberts, A., Donaldson, J., & Coxe, A. C. (1997). *The Ante-Nicene Fathers Vol.I : Translations of the writings of the Fathers down to A.D. 325.* The apostolic fathers with Justin Martyr and Irenaeus. (246). Oak Harbor: Logos Research Systems. Justin *Dialogue with Trypho* chapter 94.

to Christ: "Then I replied, 'Just as God commanded the sign to be made by the brazen serpent, and yet He is blameless; even so, though a curse lies in the law against persons who are crucified, yet no curse lies on the Christ of God, by whom all that have committed things worthy of a curse are saved.'"[240]

The debate between Justin and Trypho shows that the biggest offense to the Jews was the Christian claim that the King of the Jews had come into history and was crucified. This also is shown by the often repeated citation of Psalm 110:1 (in whole or in part, or by allusion) in the New Testament. It was the early Christians' answer to how Christ could have come and died, and yet still reign on the throne. Peter, on the day of Pentecost, used Psalm 110:1 in the first Christian sermon ever preached to a Jewish audience. He argued that since the Holy One of God cannot suffer decay (Psalm 16:10) and that David was still buried in a tomb, that therefore the promise must apply to someone else. Since Christ was raised from the dead and bodily ascended into heaven, He is the Holy One of God, the greater son of David who would reign. But why didn't Jesus defeat Israel's enemies as the prophets said that Messiah would? Here is Peter's answer from Psalm 110:1:

> For it was not David who ascended into heaven, but he himself says: "The Lord said to my Lord, 'Sit at My right hand, Until I make Thine enemies a footstool for Thy feet.'" Therefore let all the house of Israel know for certain that God has made Him both Lord and Christ—this Jesus whom you crucified. (**Acts 2:34 – 36**)

Even Jesus had cited Psalm 110:1, asking His critics how the "son of David" could also be the Lord of David (Matthew 22:42-45). Jesus is indeed the Davidic king being David's Lord who sits on the throne in heaven at God's right hand.

That Jesus is seated at the right hand of God as predicted in Psalm 110:1 is mentioned 19 times in the New Testament.[241]

240 Ibid.

241 Matt. 22:44; 26:64; Mark 12:36; 14:62; Luke 20:42; 22:69; Acts 2:34; 5:31; 7:55, 56; Rom. 8:34; Eph. 1:20; Col. 3:1; Heb. 1:3; 1:13; 8:1; 10:12; 12:2; 1Peter 3:22.

But there is an "until" in Psalm 110:1. The role of defeating Israel's (and God's) enemies is postponed, but not abrogated. Though Jesus is indeed reigning on the throne, His enemies freely blaspheme Him with apparent impunity. People routinely curse Christ and mock His word, and many still live long and happy lives. (Once, an apostate who is now an atheist told me that his life has been long and happy since he renounced Christ and embraced atheism.) So what happens between Christ's ascending to sit on the throne in heaven and His descending to destroy His enemies? The answer will help us understand the Biblical doctrine of the kingdom of God. Emergent/postmodern teachers obscure this doctrine and convince their followers that a rosy future, free of judgment or wrath, awaits them.

HOW THE KINGDOM GAINS CITIZENS

The Emergent/postmodern approach, as we have seen, sees the kingdom in good works or in a community that shares social values and tries to spread them in the world. But the idea of God's reign is central to any definition of the kingdom, as is the identity of the king. We have seen that Jesus is the king and that He is reigning from the right hand of God in heaven. But who or what does he reign over? Is His reign found somewhere on earth by looking for certain characteristics as Pagitt claimed? Not according to the Bible.

The first issue is to determine the terms of entrance into the kingdom. We mentioned in an earlier chapter that John's gospel teaches that one must be born again in order to see or enter the kingdom (John 3:3-5). In a very important passage, Mark describes the beginning of Jesus' ministry this way: "*And after John had been taken into custody, Jesus came into Galilee, preaching the gospel of God, and saying, 'The time is fulfilled, and the kingdom of God is at hand; repent and believe in the gospel'*" (Mark 1:14, 15). The presence of the promised King on the scene of history created a crisis. The Greek term used here for "time" (*kairos*) denotes "the crucial moment." The nearness of the kingdom was a threat to unrepentant sinners. The call to "repent and believe" is a call to respond in faith and turn to God on His terms, which is faith in Christ.

William Lane's commentary explains this passage well:

> The brief parable of the fig tree preserved by Mark in Ch. 13:28 echoes Jesus' proclamation that the kingdom *has come near* and clarifies why the nearness of the kingdom imposes radical demands upon men: "When the branch becomes tender and the leave are about to sprout, you know that the summer *has come near*"; i.e., the summer is *the next thing* that comes. Jesus' action in confronting Satan, sin, disease and death, and subduing nature is the sign that the end stands as the next act of God in man's future. Provision has been made for men to repent, but there is no time for delay.[242]

The arrival of the kingdom will be very bad news for God's enemies, and all sinners are God's enemies. We are in the crucial moment now that Jesus has come and completed His work, and only those who repent and believe become citizens of the kingdom. Lane explains, "*Either* a man submits to the summons of God *or* he chooses this world and its riches and honor. The either/or character of this decision is of immense importance and permits of no postponement."[243]

Jesus said many shocking things about entrance to the kingdom. For example: "*For I say to you, that unless your righteousness surpasses that of the scribes and Pharisees, you shall not enter the kingdom of heaven*" (**Matthew 5:20**). Not even the most scrupulous religious leaders had the righteousness necessary to enter. The "righteous" in Matthew are also called "sons of the kingdom," those who are right with God because of having submitted to Christ who is the King. Consider this passage:

> *And He answered* [a request to explain the parable of the tares] *and said, "The one who sows the good seed is the Son of Man, and the field is the world; and as for the good seed, these are the sons of the kingdom; and the tares are the sons of*

242 William Lane, "The Gospel of Mark," in *The New International Commentary on the New Testament* (Grand Rapids: Eerdmans, 1974) 66.

243 Ibid.

> *the evil one; and the enemy who sowed them is the devil, and the harvest is the end of the age; and the reapers are angels. Therefore just as the tares are gathered up and burned with fire, so shall it be at the end of the age. The Son of Man will send forth His angels, and they will gather out of His kingdom all stumbling blocks, and those who commit lawlessness, and will cast them into the furnace of fire; in that place there shall be weeping and gnashing of teeth. Then the righteous will shine forth as the sun in the kingdom of their Father. He who has ears, let him hear."* (**Matthew 13:37 – 43**)

This section of Matthew disproves the use of the phrase "kingdom of God" by Emergent/postmodern leaders. They deny the reality of future judgment where some people are cast into hell. They claim that the kingdom is something that comes to earth through a process of people helping God re-create the world. That is not what Jesus taught.

All through church history, from Pentecost onward, people are being summoned to submit to the reign of the King enthroned in heaven. They are told that He will return and all of His enemies will become a footstool for His feet (meaning they will be defeated and judged). The parable of the tares makes it clear that this happens at the end of the age, not through an ongoing process within history. The issue is whether we submit to God's reign by repenting and believing the gospel, thus becoming "sons of the kingdom," or whether we stay as we are and prove to be tares, sons of the evil one, to be cast into the fire at the end of the age.

In Luke 19 a parable explains the issue of the already/not yet aspects of the kingdom. It begins this way: "*And while they were listening to these things, He went on to tell a parable, because He was near Jerusalem, and they supposed that the kingdom of God was going to appear immediately. He said therefore, 'A certain nobleman went to a distant country to receive a kingdom for himself, and then return'*" (**Luke 19:11, 12**). This is about the period of time between the first and second advents of Christ. The next verses show the key issue: "*And he called ten of his slaves, and gave them ten minas, and said to them, 'Do business with this until I come back.' But his citizens hated him, and sent a delegation after him, saying, 'We do not want* *this man to reign over us*'" (**Luke 19:13, 14**). Jesus reigns at the right hand of God until he returns to defeat his enemies. Throughout church history the terms of the gospel are being preached. People have to decide if they want Jesus to reign over them or not. Will they repent? In the parable, when the master returns, He gives his servants various rewards. But this is what happens to those who will not submit to Christ: "*But these enemies of mine, who did not want me to reign over them, bring them here and slay them in my presence*" (**Luke 19:27**).

The kingdom gains citizens as individuals repent and believe the gospel; those who repent come under the reign of King Jesus and are now citizens of heaven. Paul tells the Christians in Colossae: "*For He delivered us from the domain of darkness, and transferred us to the kingdom of His beloved Son*" (**Colossians 1:13**). He told the Philippians:

> *For many walk, of whom I often told you, and now tell you even weeping, that they are enemies of the cross of Christ, whose end is destruction, whose god is their appetite, and whose glory is in their shame, who set their minds on earthly things. For our citizenship is in heaven, from which also we eagerly wait for a Savior, the Lord Jesus Christ; who will transform the body of our humble state into conformity with the body of His glory, by the exertion of the power that He has even to subject all things to Himself.* (**Philippians 3:18 – 21**)

Emergent/postmodern theology loathes talk about heaven, future judgment, and escaping the corruption of this present evil age. But the clear teaching of the Bible emphasizes these things. No wonder they claim we cannot know what the Bible says.

THE RIGHTEOUSNESS OF CHRIST

The righteousness that exceeds that of the Scribes and Pharisees is the imputed righteousness of Christ. Without that righteousness no one will enter the kingdom of God. That righteousness is available only because of the substitutionary atonement, which most in the Emergent Church deny. So ironically, while calling themselves "kingdom-oriented" they refuse to teach the only means by which anyone can enter the kingdom. Entering the kingdom does not happen by human acts of benevolence. It requires a supernatural act of God: "*And again I say to you, it is easier for a camel to go through the eye of a needle, than for a rich man to enter the kingdom of God. And when the disciples heard this, they were very astonished and said, 'Then who can be saved?' And looking upon them Jesus said to them, 'With men this is impossible, but with God all things are possible*'" (**Matthew 19:24 – 26**).

In the next chapter we shall explore the philosophical source of Emergent/postmodern thinking. We shall see that like the theological source examined in the first chapter, the philosophical source leads back to Fredrick Hegel.

Abstract Chapter 9

EMERGENCE Theory—The Philosophical Source of Emergent Theology

MOLTMANN'S THEOLOGY + WILBER'S PHILOSOPHY = EMERGENT

We began by showing theologian Jürgen Moltmann to be the source of Emergent's eschatology. We will conclude by showing that Ken Wilber is the source of Emergent philosophy. Both their theology and philosophy contend that everyone must be headed toward a future utopia with God. Wilber describes a philosophical framework for the idea of "emergence" by describing an upward spiral, whereby everything is evolving into something better. Wilber is rather a mystical Darwin, promoting a "holistic" concept of evolution in which things are not only evolving physically but also spiritually. This spiritual evolution is the basis of "spiral dynamics," where the world evolves into a physical/spiritual paradise over time.

THE PAGAN WORLDVIEW REPACKAGED IN CHRISTIAN TERMINOLOGY

Wilber is a neo-Buddhist, and his philosophy "absorbs" pagan and Christian concepts into one unified view of spirituality. His arguments seek "essentials" to spirituality, mysticism, paganism, and Christianity, and he combines them into "holistic" values that also evolve into something better and more mature. The details of Wilber's thought are difficult for someone outside of his philosophy even to understand. One reason is that Wilber created his own language that works with his ideas and concepts. Do not be concerned if his arguments seem strange and difficult to understand—they are. Philosophical paganism is a difficult concept for anyone to make understandable or plausible.

HEGEL AGAIN, AND AGAIN

What is most important to learn from this chapter is that Wilber's philosophy also has its roots in Hegel, the same philosopher from whom Moltmann drew his "theology of hope." In some sense, Hegel's belief in a synthesis where opposites like good and evil combine to form a better, third option is the root of both Wilber and Moltmann. These men, Moltmann and Wilber, and their belief in a world where everything gets better and ends in utopia are the sources of the Emergent church. Really, there is nothing unique or special about the Emergent church. Emergent simply is what a church would look like if it rejected the scriptures and looked to Hegel as its prophet. Similarly, the Mormon Church is what Christianity looks like when it rejects scripture and looks to Joseph Smith as its prophet.

The bedrock question for those who would become Emergent is whether or not the Hegelian synthesis is true. If it is not, and the Scriptures are true, they will not find the kingdom of God. They will face judgment.

9

Emergence Theory: The Philosophical Source of Emergent Theology

In chapter 1 we surveyed the theological source of Emergent/postmodern eschatology, found most directly in the writings of the German theologian Jürgen Moltmann. We shall now turn to the philosophical source of this eschatology that defines the movement. That source is found in the Integral Theory of Ken Wilber, with related ideas such as spiral dynamics and the "integral movement." These ideas are complex and very difficult for most people to grasp. But the bottom line is that it will bring us back to the eschatology of the Emergent Church: that everything is headed toward a better future that God and all He created will share.

Before we examine these ideas let us reset the stage in the discussion begun in chapter 1. Tony Jones explains this eschatology's centrality: "So I've poked around, trying to figure out exactly what's going on in the emerging church, and in Emergent Village in particular. And if there's one core conviction that I can put my finger on, it's an *eschatology of hope*."[244] We have seen how their eschatology influences most of their other beliefs and practices. We have also seen that the theological source of this eschatology came primarily from a

244 Tony Jones, "A Hopeful Faith," in *An Emergent Manifesto of Hope* Doug Pagitt and Tony Jones editors (Grand Rapids: Baker, 2007) 130.

theologian who based his own ideas on the work German philosopher Georg Wilhelm Friedrich Hegel. Hegel's ideas suggest that processes in history synthesize into something better. Jones and many others have rejected the Biblical idea that God's judgment lies in the future. Here is how he states this: "What I mean is that the folks who hang around the emerging church tend to see goodness and light in God's future, not darkness and gnashing of teeth."[245] He then summarily dismisses "the view that we're in a downward spiral, and when things 'down here' become bad enough, Jesus will return in glory."[246]

THE PHILOSOPHY OF KEN WILBER

In rejecting a "downward spiral" (that history is heading toward God's judgment), emergent/postmodern theology holds to an upward spiral theory called spiral dynamics and a helical theory of time:

> First, it [a helical structure] has a spiral form. The motion of time, the motion of life, is not linear, but spiral. Mate a line with a circle, connect linear to non-linear, connect analytic to associative powers of the brain, connect past to future–and you end up with a spiral. In spiral dynamics, each level of the past remains curled up inside us (like nested Russian dolls) as we move up to next-level challenges. A spiraling faith is one of timelessness within time, one in which the past is embedded in the future.[247]

These ideas are primarily Wilber's expressions drawn together from people such as Arthur Koesler and his concept of "holons", Alfred North Whitehead's process philosophy, and the much earlier thinking of Hegel himself. This material quickly can become very dense and confusing, but the basic idea behind it is the idea of evolution (and not just biological evolution,[248] but a holistic evolution that includes all things). It is sup-

245 Ibid.

246 Ibid.

247 Leonard Sweet, Brian McLaren, and Jerry Haselmayer, *A is for Abductive – The Language of the Emerging Church* (Grand Rapids: Zondervan, 2003). 143.

248 Ken Wilber actually criticizes biological evolution.

ported by a pantheistic worldview (Wilber being a Buddhist).[249] If God is part of the process of history, and if all of reality is interconnected, then the process can be expected to be spiraling upward to something better. This worldview is characteristic of neo-paganism in its many expressions.

It is difficult to describe these ideas without leading the reader into confusion, and any such result is unintentional. This philosophy is based on a paradigm involving life, categories, and terminology that may not correspond to anything in the real world. For example, consider the term "holons." In *A is for Abductive*, Leonard Sweet, Brian McLaren and Jerry Haselmayer discuss it: "Holarchy: The ordering (arche) of holons (whole/parts). The word holon was invented by Arthur Koestler to describe increasing levels of wholeness in the universe. Every whole is a part and every part is a whole. Everything is a holon."[250] This confusing paradigm is one of the key concepts Wilber uses; his philosophy has been adapted by the Emergent Church, and his work is footnoted in their entry.

But scientists did not discover "holons"; Koestler proposed them in his book *The Ghost in the Machine* as a way of proposing and explaining that man's brain became confounded in the evolutionary process, and thus caused the evils in society. I am not saying that Wilber's or the Emergent's use of the concept is identical to Koestler's. Koestler thought the best way to fix man's brain, wired wrongly by evolution, was through drugs. Instead of drugs, the emergent panentheism sees the immanence of God in the process as reason for hope. Wilber's Buddhist pantheistic "hope" is based on some concept of God, but it is not the God of the Bible. Theirs is a more pagan view.

My intent is to provide a basic overview of Wilber's ideas by citing both his writings and an interview he granted. His ideas are esoteric, so do not be shocked if they do not make sense to you. But since Wilber is a key source of the concept of the "emergence" underlying the philosophy of the Emergent Church, it is necessary to explain his ideas. We will find his neo-pagan ideas to be shockingly antithetical to Christian theol-

249 Ken Wilber is a pantheist but the Emergent writers who use his material are panentheistic. The difference is that panentheism still maintains a distinction between the creator and creation, believing the creation is infused with God; but that God still has His own identity. Pantheism is monistic.

250 Sweet, *Abductive*, 145.

ogy. Here is an example where he describes "emergence" and evolution according to his idea, the "Great Nest of Being":

> But, according to the traditions, this entire process of *evolution* or "un-folding" could never occur without a prior process of *involution* or "in-folding." Not only can the higher not be explained in terms of the lower, and not only does the higher not actually emerge "out of" the lower, but the reverse of both of those is true, according to the traditions. That is, the lower dimensions or levels are actually sediments or deposits of the higher dimensions, and they find their meaning because of the higher dimensions of which they are a stepped-down or diluted version. This sedimentation process is called "**involution"** or "**emanation**." According to the traditions, before evolution or the unfolding of Spirit can occur, involution or the infolding of Spirit must occur: the higher successively steps down into the lower. Thus, the higher levels appear to emerge "out of" the lower levels during evolution–for example, life appears to emerge out of matter–because, and only because, they were first deposited there by involution. You cannot get the higher out of the lower unless the higher were already there, in potential–sleeping, as it were–waiting to emerge. The "miracle of emergence" is simply Spirit's creative play in the fields of its own manifestation.[251]

The "traditions" he refers to are various versions of the "Great Chain of Being." He includes a chart that shows his conception of how this works in various religions. But take note, as a Buddhist and a pantheist, Wilber's "infolding of Spirit" is a description of Spirit being lost in the material. Here is Wilber's description in his own words: "These levels in the Great Nest are all *forms of Spirit*, but the forms become less and less conscious, less and less aware of their Source and Suchness, less and less

---

251 Cited from http://wilber.shambhala.com/html/books/kosmos/excerptG/part1.cfm This is an excerpt from a draft of a book Wilber is writing called Kosmic Karma. (accessed April, 2008)

alive to their ever-present Ground, even though they are all nevertheless nothing but Spirit-at-play."[252] So all things are "Spirit at play" but have lost awareness of this. Evolution is Spirit manifesting itself in emerging levels of complexity and awareness. The reason evolution makes sense in this scheme is that either God is in the creation (panentheism) or that creation is a manifestation of God (pantheism). In Christian theology, God created the world out of nothing and then rested (Genesis 1). The creation is separate from God.

But if creation is Spirit-at-play as Wilber says, there is reason to think that things can evolve into more complex and better realities. Here is his explanation of the involution process that is subsequently reversed to be evolution:

> Spirit "loses" itself, "forgets" itself, takes on a magical façade of manyness (*maya*) in order to have a grand game of hide-and-seek with itself. Spirit first throws itself outward to create soul, which is a stepped-down and diluted reflection of Spirit; soul then steps down into mind, a paler reflection yet of Spirit's radiant glory; mind then steps down into life, and life steps down into matter, which is the densest, lowest, least conscious form of Spirit. We might represent this as: Spirit-as-spirit steps down into Spirit-as-soul, which steps down into Spirit-as-mind, which steps down into Spirit-as-body, which steps down into Spirit-as-matter. These levels in the Great Nest are all *forms of Spirit*, but the forms become less and less conscious, less and less aware of their Source and Suchness, less and less alive to their ever-present Ground, even though they are all nevertheless nothing but Spirit-at-play.[253]

So whatever sort of "deity" Spirit is in this scheme of things, either he or "it" as the case may be, it has lost consciousness of its own existence and must regain consciousness. This is where we come in. We are supposed to

252 Ibid.
253 Ibid.

help the emergence of Kosmic[254] consciousness through meditation. In essence, we help God find himself. I find it interesting that Wilber cites Hegel approvingly: "But the traditionalists were more straightforward about it: 'God does not remain petrified and dead; the very stones cry out and raise themselves to Spirit,' as Hegel put it."[255]

Wilber says "traditionalists" because though he admires their experiences and ideas, he wants to synthesize them into a better version of the Great Chain of Being that will incorporate more ideas: "It is not so much that the scheme itself is wrong, as that the modern and postmodern world has added several profound insights that need to be added or incorporated if we want a more integral or comprehensive view. This is what is meant by 'from the Great Chain to postmodernism in three easy steps.'"[256] Then Wilber proceeds to point out the shortcomings of pre-modern meta-physics, modern meta-physics, and propose an integration of pre-modern, modern, and postmodern understandings using a quadrant theory he proposes.[257]

What Wilber proposes is that all evolving exterior things have a corresponding interior aspect which also is evolving. So rather than being "meta-physical" (concerned with things that transcend physics, and therefore would be considered beyond or above physics such as questions of causality, the ultimate nature of being and so forth) he considers them "intra-physical." In this scheme, every form of reality, including atoms, has a corresponding interior, spiritual reality (as understood by panentheism or pantheism). This is reflected in Wilber's quadrants. Furthermore, the exterior and interior realities that evolve into higher levels of complexity have a correspondence to social realities, both of individuals and society. Thus the quadrants are "I, we, it, its." These are for "interior individual, exterior individual, interior collective and exterior collective." All are evolving in complexity in both interior and exterior aspects, but evolution incorporates everything that went before and does not leave anything behind.

---

254 Wilber purposely spells "cosmic" as "kosmic" to distinguish his ideas from the idea of the cosmos which is usually not referenced in a pantheistic way but can mean "creation."

255 Ibid.

256 Ibid.

257 The best way to understand this is to go to his Web site http://wilber.shambhala.com/ and look at the charts and representations there. But all of it is based on his Buddhist world-view, the lens through which he integrates everything else.

I realize this is complex, but it is necessary to understand because it is the source of much of Emergent leadership's thinking—such as McLaren's and Rob Bell's. I can only demonstrate it by first helping you to understand Wilber. In his pantheistic thinking, all of reality, including the atomic level, is spiritual and has consciousness. Here is his explanation: "But each of those material forms of *increasing complexity* has, as an *interior* correlate, a level of *increasing consciousness*. Thus (following Whitehead): atoms, whose exterior forms are physical entities such as neutrons, protons, and electrons, have an interior of prehension or proto-feelings (proto-awareness). . ."[258] Of course, this makes sense to Wilber because of his Buddhist worldview. Fritjof Capra, whose book *The Tao of Physics* uses quantum physics to support a monistic, Eastern meta-physic, is mentioned by Wilber, who criticizes him for "reducing all realities to one quadrant." But the idea that everything is spiritual in some sense is also Capra's idea.

Wilber claims that evolution includes the external and internal, or the matter and consciousness:

> *Increasing complexity of form (in the UR) is correlated with increasing interior consciousness (in the UL).* This was Teilhard de Chardin's "law of complexity and consciousness"—namely, the more of the former, the more of the latter. As we might put it more precisely, the greater the degree of exterior complexity of material form, the greater the degree of interior consciousness that can be enacted within that form (i.e., correlation of UR and UL).[259]

The UR and UL designations refer to his quadrant scheme, upper right and upper left. If one keys "evolving consciousness" into Google.com, the Web sites that appear include a veritable who's who of New Age thinkers, including Wilber.[260]

258 Wilber *Kosmic Karma* excerpt.

259 Ibid.

260 This site: http://www.wie.org/directory/evolution-consciousness.asp which is "What is Enlightenment, Redefining Spirituality for an Evolving World," is filled with links and articles including material by Ken Wilber. (accessed April, 2008)

Other terms and ideas associated with Wilber exist, but his quadrant map of reality is at the heart of them. Other terms include spiral dynamics, holarchy, integral dynamics, and integral theory of consciousness.

Wilber has been interviewed frequently, and though he offers his comprehensive philosophy in his books, he claims they are not intended to help with the "advancement of consciousness." When asked what knowing his philosophy could do for the advancement of consciousness[261] he replied,

> Not very much, frankly. Each of us still has to find a genuine contemplative practice–maybe yoga, maybe Zen, maybe Shambhala Training, maybe contemplative prayer, or any number or authentic transformative practices. That is what advances consciousness, not my linguistic chitchat and book junk.[262]

Meditation advances consciousness, he says, even in the absence of understanding his integral theory. No wonder various versions of meditation are popular in Emergent Churches.

Understanding this theory is not for the faint of heart. A further exchange in the interview: "Your own world view is complicated enough. Meditators might just say, 'Why do I need to have a global-historical view at all? Leave me alone to just meditate.' What would you say to them?" Wilber's answer: "Just meditate."[263] The interview reveals Wilber's highest regard for Buddhist mediation, whose goal is to reach emptiness.

At one point, the interview turned to what Wilber termed, "mystical Christianity". The question posed was why a thousand years of it had not delivered "transcendence". His response:

> Imagine if, the very day Buddha attained his enlightenment, he was taken out and hanged precisely because of his realization. And if any of his followers

---

261 "The Kosmos According to Ken Wilber - A Dialogue with Robin Korman" in Shambhala Sun September 1996: http://www.shambhalasun.com/index.php?option=com_content&task=view&id=2059 (accessed April 2, 2008).

262 Ibid.

263 Ibid.

> claimed to have the same realization, they were also hanged. Speaking for myself, I would find this something of a disincentive to practice. But that's exactly what happened with Jesus of Nazareth. "Why do you stone me?" he asks at one point. "Is it for good deeds?" And the crowd responds, "No, it is because you, being a man, make yourself out to be God." The individual Atman is not allowed to realize that it is one with Brahman. "I and my Father are One"-among other complicated factors-that realization got this gentleman crucified. The reasons for this are involved, but the fact remains: as soon as any spiritual practitioner began to get too close to the realization that Atman and Brahman are one—that one's own mind is intrinsically one with primordial Spirit-then frighteningly severe repercussions usually followed.[264]

Wilber interprets Christ to be an early Buddha type who was crucified for holding Buddhist ideas.

Needless to say, Ken Wilber's ideas are antithetical to the teachings of the Bible. Why would Christian theologians and teachers look to them for guidance? The answer is that they are interested in "emergence", and Wilber is a brilliant philosopher whose combination of physical and spiritual evolution points to a better future through meditation.

KEN WILBER'S IDEAS IN THE EMERGENT CHURCH

McLaren devoted an entire chapter to emergent thinking in *a Generous Orthodoxy* ("Why I Am Emergent"—chapter 19). In it he claims he is influenced by Ken Wilber in significant ways: "In this chapter I am trying (with Ken Wilber's help) to make clear that I believe there is something above and beyond the current alternatives of modern fundamentalism/ absolutism *and* pluralistic relativism. . . . This 'above and beyond' is, I believe the way of Jesus, which is the way of love and embrace. It integrates what has gone before so that something new can emerge."[265] This

---

264 Ibid.

265 Brian McLaren, *a Generous Orthodoxy* (El Cajon, CA: Youth Specialties, 2004; published by Zondervan) 287.

is indeed a good summary of Wilber's integral theory. And as we saw, Wilber claimed that Jesus had ideas like his. This "above and beyond" that emerges also fits the scheme of the Hegelian synthesis.

McLaren uses the rings of a tree to illustrate the idea of everything having gone before being incorporated into what is, using what comes from below and from above.[266] The tree even incorporates "remnants of its ancestors–their leaves and wood recycled through decomposition."[267] This illustrates the type of thinking McLaren embraces: "But some thought seeks to embrace what has come before–like a new ring on a tree–in something bigger. This is *emergent* (or integral, or integrative) thinking. Emergent thinking has been an unspoken assumption behind all my previous books."[268] This scheme of thinking smacks of Ken Wilber's philosophy–very much so.

McLaren also embraces the concept of the Great Chain of Being that is so important to Wilber's thinking: "The 'Great Chain of Being' (better called, says integral philosopher Ken Wilber, the 'Great Nest of Being') seeks to capture this emergence."[269] McLaren then traces this from space and time through inanimate matter, microbiotic plant life, animal life, human life, and spiritual life. Wilber illustrated this scheme in his four-quadrant theory. McLaren writes, "Spiritual life [is]: the domain of awareness of God, accessed through theology and spirituality and mysticicsm, which encompasses domains 1 through 5, and adds the experience of the sacred and conscious relationship with God."[270] Again, this hardly deviates from Wilber's philosophy as we described it above. Wilber's previously cited work contains a ring diagram (like McLaren's tree rings) and categories precisely like McLaren's and is entitled *The Traditional Great Chain of Being*.[271]

The idea of holons (Wilber's version) shows up in McLaren's writings as well. In the entry under "emergence" in *A is for Abductive*, McLaren and his co-authors write, "When 'perturbations' take place, the self-organizing system is shaken up and begins to reshuffle the deck.

---

266 Ibid. 277.
267 Ibid.
268 Ibid. 278.
269 Ibid. 279.
270 Ibid. 280.
271 Wilber, *Kosmic Karma* excerpt.

New connections are made and new holons emerge."[272] Wilber's writings describe this in great detail. The Esalen Center Web site offers a summary of Wilber's "Twenty Tenets" that describes how holons are part of the evolutionary process in this scheme of reality.[273] The following are summaries of some of the twenty points:

3. Holons emerge.
4. Holons emerge holarchically.
5. Each holon transcends and includes its predecessors.
6. The lower sets the possibilities of the higher; the higher sets the probabilities of the lower.
7. The number of levels which a hierarchy comprises determines whether it is 'shallow' or 'deep;' and the number of holons on any given level we shall call its 'span.'
8. Each successive level of evolution produces greater depth and less span.
9. Destroy any type of holon, and you will destroy all of the holons above it and none of the holons below it.
10. Holarchies co-evolve. The micro is always within the macro (all agency is agency in communion).

McLaren and co-authors also discuss "holarchy" in an entry by that title in their book: "There is a sacred order to the universe and its web of relationships that combines both hierarchy and heterarchy. It is called *holarchy*."[274] The entry explains the idea and cites Koestler and Wilber.

I am not writing about this to establish an invalid guilt by association. If McLaren and other emergent/postmodern writers cited Wilber positively about some point it would not prove that they agree with his philosophy. But in this case they *do* believe it, promote it, and repeat it–including using the terminology the same way he does. They cite Wilber as the source. The bigger question is whether or not Wilber's Buddhist philosophy can be integrated into a version of Christianity. My answer? Not without destroying a biblical worldview. Jesus was not,

272 Sweet, *Abductive*, 108.

273 "Evolutionary Theory, An Esalen Invitational Conference, Ken Wilber's Twenty Tenets" by George Leonard: http://www.esalenctr.org/display/confpage.cfm?confid=10&pageid=113&pgtype=1 (accessed April, 2008)

274 Sweet, *Abductive*, 144.

as Wilber claims, a forerunner to Buddha who happened to get himself killed because of his ideas!

McLaren identifies the evolution of matter and spirit, with holons (parts that make up the bigger whole that are incorporated into what has evolved and will be incorporated into what is evolving) as that which is ultimately the kingdom of God. He says, "Similar diagrams could picture individuals in families, in communities, in cultures, in a world, in God's kingdom."[275] Using Wilber's "nest" idea from his Great Nest of Being, McLaren reasons, "All things are nested in a larger reality, and the largest reality, the one that comprises them, the ultimate domain is, I believe, what Jesus meant when he announced 'The kingdom (or domain) of God.'"[276] This reasoning is hardly superior to Wilber's idea that Jesus was a Buddha-type who had realized that Atman was one with Brahman. A speculative theory based on holons, holarchy, the Great Chain of Being reinterpreted, and the Great Nest of Being was hardly what Jesus spoke about in the gospels.

What is truly amazing is McLaren's definition of "sin" that corresponds to emergent theory and Wilber's Great Nest of Being:

> Sin, in this model, can be understood as lower levels or rings resisting the emergence of higher levels or rings, body-lusts refusing to be integrated with mental ideals in an ethical soul; individual wills (a mental faculty) refusing to develop the virtues of soul necessary so that healthy families and communities and cultures can emerge; individual kingdoms (which we could call we-isms) refusing to yield territory to the emergence of the larger (and largest reality)-God's kingdom (which we could call good theism).[277]

McLaren holds so many of Wilber's ideas that one is surprised to learn that he doesn't include Wilber's quadrant chart in his book. Sin is anything, or anyone, who resists the process of spiritual evolution. It is obvious that conservative Christians like me—those who warn people about

275 McLaren, *Generous*, 281.
276 Ibid.
277 Ibid.

this as I am doing in this book—are the biggest sinners of all. But the Biblical definition of sin is not to resist cosmic evolution, but to transgress God's moral law. The process of evolution can have setbacks, according to emergence theory, but it inevitably reorganizes and moves forward. Sin then is whatever causes a setback or slows down the process. Says McLaren, "Because of this counter-emergent virus we call sin, the stages, episodes, and levels don't always unfold as they should."[278]

In *A is for Abductive*, Sweet, McLaren and Haselmayer even suggest the end of entropy. In the entry under Eschaton in a section entitled "The End of Entropy" they write, "In the postmodern matrix there is a good chance that the world will reverse its chronological polarity for us. Instead of being bound to the past by chains of cause and effect, we will feel ourselves being pulled into the future by the magnet of God's will, God's dream, God's desire."[279] So, accordingly, rather than the universe winding down due to heat loss, and history headed toward future judgment, things are getting better as we are head back (which is now forward) toward paradise.

As we consider these ideas we need to remember what we learned in Chapter 7 about coherentism. I pointed out that the key reason for rejecting foundationalism is to detach one's system of belief from the real world. Once detached, the worldview holds together internally as it floats in a sea of subjectivity. McLaren and co-authors do not offer any evidence for the end of entropy or the reversal of time "polarity." For example, if entropy ended, it would be immediately possible to create a perpetual motion machine because available energy would no longer be degrading. But rather than dazzle the scientific world by creating such a machine and proving their ideas (which they cannot), they simply incorporate those ideas into a coherent whole that floats detached from the real world.

The same can be said for Wilber's philosophy. He is brilliant, and his ideas cohere within his own system of thought. But is coherence a valid test for truth? Postmodern thinkers claim it is. But the universe is what it is and is totally unaffected by human philosophy. No evidence in history supports their hypothesis that the universe is evolving in the manner these men claim. In fact, what we see in the real world is best

278 Ibid. 282.

279 Sweet, *Abductive*, 113.

accounted for by the Biblical doctrine of creation of man in God's image followed by the Fall of man.

In *He is There and He Is Not Silent* Francis Schaeffer argued persuasively that the Bible's claims are true to the real world in which we live; what he termed "paneverythingism" is not. (Schaeffer did not think that pantheism deserved to have "theism" in its title.) Schaeffer claimed that the Bible as special revelation and everything observable as general revelation speak as one at the point of metaphysics.[280] He warned about the very thing McLaren and other postmodern thinkers are now doing:

> But if we are going to have this answer [that Christianity is true to what God said in the Bible and to the real world we live in], notice that we must have the *full biblical* answer, and not reduce Christianity to either the paneverythingism of the East, or the paneverythingism of modern, liberal theology, whether Protestant or Roman Catholic. We *must not* reduce Christianity to the modern existential, upper-story theology.[281]

By following the emergence theory of pantheist Ken Wilber and proposing ideas that are both unbiblical and unscientific, McLaren and company have done just what Schaeffer warned us not to do. There is no more evidence for Wilber's Kosmic evolution than there ever was for biological evolution.

These ideas are not new. Theologian Bernard Ramm wrote about Hegel's idea of evolution:

> The German philosopher Georg Hegel (1770-1831) proposed a comprehensive philosophical theory of evolution before Charles Darwin suggested a biological one. His scheme of evolution of *Geist* (Mind, Spirit) was one of the grandest in the history of philosophy. It centered in the development of the different branches of human culture (art, religion, politics, philosophy) and presumed they each had the shape

280 Francis A. Schaefer, *He is There and He is Not Silent*, (Wheaton: Tyndale, 1972) 18.
281 Ibid.

> of an ever upward-moving spiral. Each point on the spiral higher than previous points was *Geist* coming to a fuller clarification. In this upward spiraling there had to be critical transition points where lower elements were caught up and reconciled in a higher synthesis. . . . This spiral pattern applies to human moral and religious development.[282]

It is easy to see that Wilber's ideas are similar to Hegel's—and are more comprehensive. Thus Wilber speaks of "spiral dynamics."

But these ideas, as we saw in McLaren, are not compatible with the Biblical doctrine of sin and the Fall. The Bible teaches that the horrid consequences of sin are played out in the evils resident in human history and that sin must come under God's judgment: That judgment falls either upon Christ, who was the perfect, sinless sacrifice for sin, or it will fall on unredeemed humans who refuse to repent and believe the gospel. But because of God's perfect justice, the judgment cannot be averted without Christ's shed blood. But as we are learning, Emergent/postmodern theology rejects both the substitutionary atonement and literal future judgment.

Here is Hegel's view of the Fall, as explained by Ramm:

> Humankind is differentiated from animals through possessing a moral consciousness. By sinning, humanity made the transition from the premoral state of innocence to moral consciousness. In effect, humanity fell upward. Hegel agreed with Kant that Gen. 3 could be accepted if interpreted symbolically or mythologically, but in his system the Fall of Gen. 3 moved up the spiral. . . . This view of sin received a good hearing among some theologians of liberal Christianity. Insofar as they too rejected the historic doctrines of the Fall, Original Sin, and Depravity, they needed a theory of human sinning to account for the blatant facts of human depravity.[283]

---

282 Bernard Ramm, *Offense to Reason – The Theology of Sin*; (New York: Harper and Row, 1985) 16, 17.

283 Ibid. 17.

Things are even worse now because "blatant facts," whether Biblical or from general revelation, are no longer important to postmodern theologians. In chapter 1 we saw Hegel as a primary source of the theology of the Emergent Church, now we see that he is also a key source of their philosophy.

For example, consider how McLaren and co-authors describe their idea of emergence: "Emergence theory incorporates into an intellectual and spiritual framework ancient and recent arguments for intelligent design (focusing on diversity and complexity) with certain aspects of evolution (natural selection and the fossil record). In this view, part of the goodness of Creation is an inherent potential to generate new possibilities so that more and more goodness can emerge."[284] Notice that what "emerges" is goodness which is a moral category. This is not a Biblical explanation of creation followed by the Fall that explains both good and evil, but philosophical speculation after the manner of Ken Wilber. Goodness does not emerge; as Jesus said: "only God is good." But if you have a panentheistic or pantheistic system, God is part of the process, thus goodness can be deemed to "emerge."

The same ideas can be seen in Rob Bell's teachings. Bell writes, "For a mind-blowing introduction to emergence theory and divine creativity, set aside three months and read Ken Wilber's *A Brief History of Everything*."[285] This is in a footnote to a section where Bell describes creation as having the built-in empowerment to produce more. Bell's ideas are not identical to Wilber's but are a modification of them. Bell writes, "Not only are we connected with creation, but creation is going to move forward. It can't help it. It is loaded with energy. It's going to grow and produce and change and morph."[286] Bell's description of the Fall also is inadequate and more in line with panentheism. Rather than rebelling against God and transgressing His moral law, Adam and Eve made a mess of the balance of things by falling out of harmony:

> God has given us power and potential and ability. God has given this power to us so we will *use it well*. We have choices about how we are going to use our power.

284 Sweet, *Abductive*, 108-109.

285 Rob Bell, *Velvet Elvis – Rethinking the Christian Faith* (Grand Rapids: Zondervan, 2005) 192 (footnote 143 from page 157).

286 Ibid. 158.

> The choices of the first people were so toxic because they were placed in the middle of a complex web of interaction and relationships with the world God had made. When they sinned, their actions threw off the balance of everything. It is all one, and when one part starts to splinter and fracture, the whole thing starts to crumble.[287]

Bell cites Romans 8:22 in a footnote about the creation groaning. But he interprets this as a system thrown off balance that we need to work to put back in balance. But in Romans 8:20 it says that God subjected the creation to "futility" and that it will be God who will change this in the future when believers are raised from the dead. Bell's interpretation has more to do with Wilber's integral theory than with the Biblical doctrines of the Fall and future judgment. In the Genesis account God cursed the earth because of man's rebellion against His moral law. The issue was not the system being thrown off balance.

In a DVD of Bell's *Everything is Spiritual* tour, one sees the same theological problems. In a very elaborate and comprehensive discussion of creation and the expanse of the universe at both the macro and micro levels, Bell comes to the conclusion that "everything is spiritual." But what does that mean? Again, his interpretations reference some Biblical concepts but they are interpreted in a panentheistic manner. He interprets sub-atomic physics in a manner reminiscent of that of the previously mentioned Fritjof Capra. Bell says: "The best we can come up with is that the universe, at its core, is some sort of relationship of energy. So you have brilliant, studied, respected research scientists saying: 'All we can come up with is that universe at its core is made up of some sort of relational energy that we simply can't control.'"[288]

But the fact that quantum mechanics yields only so much explanatory power by using mathematical equations to predict the likelihood of electrons being in certain places does not prove that everything is "relational energy". What is known is that, because of certain known things, we realize that at the smallest level parts of the universe remain unknown to us. That does not prove the type of metaphysic proposed

287 Ibid. 159.

288 Rob Bell, *Everything is Spiritual*, DVD, (Grand Rapids: Zondervan, 2007)

by Capra or that this "relational energy" is God or that "everything is spiritual." Bell cites "String Theory" which is entirely speculative: "String Theorists are saying there are at least 11 dimensions to reality."[289]

McLaren and co-authors also speculate about "string theory" to tease their readers with ideas akin to pantheism:

> The implications of this emerging theory [string theory] of course, are even harder to predict than the theory is to understand. But it is tempting to speculate that a world where matter is actually an organized form of energy must become a world more open to Spirit, a world where old dichotomies like "natural" and "supernatural" seem rather facile, and world that is once again vibrant with the voice of God whose "let there be light" (i.e., "Let there be energy") now invites a new kind of literal interpretation.[290]

This speculative thinking is very much parallel to Wilber's ideas about Spirit-at-play involved *within* and *as* the universe. To erase the distinction between natural and supernatural is to reject the distinction between the Creator and creation, with "Spirit" being a form of "relational energy" in the universe.

Bell's DVD dealing with creation and its human implications has a glaring lack: there is no mention of the Fall or human sin. It also leaves out another important category: spiritual evil and evil spirits. Bell calls all humans "spiritual" without exception. But this is contrary to Biblical usage. Paul calls those who have been born again "spiritual" and all others "carnal." The "natural man" cannot understand the things of God because they are "spiritually" discerned by those who are "spiritual" (i.e., those who believe, as in 1Corinthians 2:14, 15). In Romans 8:4-8 Paul teaches the same idea. Unbelievers are not called "spiritual" in the Bible. Bell says, "He's [Jesus] teaching them that all of life is drenched in the divine. The issue is whether our eyes are open enough to see it."[291] This was Bell's misinterpretation of Jesus' saying

---

289 Ibid.

290 Sweet, *Abductive*, 270.

291 Bell, *Everything*

about doing something for "the least of these." He forgets that Jesus was speaking of "brothers", which is not a universal category. Even if applied to people in general (which is doubtful) it does not prove that everything is "drenched in the divine," a phrase which ignores the categories of good and evil (and of creation and Creator for that matter).

In the DVD Bell makes a drawing on a white board with a "V" on top of an inverted "V" with a human figure in the middle. Within the top "V" are spiritual things and within the bottom one material things. On the figure it reads, "you are here."[292] This supports his concept of humans being the "fusion of these two realms." I saw a diagram nearly identical to this on Wilber's Web site, and it caught my attention. Wilber's diagram illustrates "a great holarchy of being and knowing" and has a "V" on top an inverted "V" on the bottom with a figure of a persons face in the middle.[293] On the outer part of the "Vs" are "infinite" on the top one and "Spirit" on the bottom. In my estimation, Bell's ideas are not identical to Wilber's but are a quasi-Christian version of very similar thinking.

At the DVD's end Bell claims, "The reality that Jesus came to announce, to die for, and to rise for, He called 'the kingdom of God.'" But do not get too excited about hearing the gospel on *Everything is Spiritual*, because this "kingdom" is not a threat to unrepentant sinners who reject Christ; it is a nice, warm and friendly "reality" that is all around us. Bell never explains why Christ would have to die in such a scheme of thinking. Bell says about the kingdom:

> We might say, "the reality of God" or "the way of God." "This reality," Jesus said, "is here. It's now, It's among us. It's upon us." Jesus never said that it's somewhere else. . . He came; essentially, to articlulate for us an integrated, holistic spirituality that everything we are looking for is not over there. It's not behind there. It's not down there. It's right here. The issue is if our eyes are open to see it. . . . And may you come to see that everything is spiritual.[294]

---

292 That diagram is on the Wikipedia entry for "Rob Bell" http://en.wikipedia.org/wiki/Rob_Bell

293 It can be viewed here: http://wilber.shambhala.com/html/books/kosmos/excerptG/part1.cfm

294 Bell, *Everything*

As we learned in chapter 8 on the kingdom of God, this ignores many important passages that indicate that universalism is false. This definition of "spiritual" is nearly identical to that of New Age talk show guests who call themselves "spiritual." This definition has nothing to do with repentance, faith, or the blood atonement. In short, it is not Christian theology, it is New Age panentheism.

In McLaren's chapter on emergence where he credits Wilber for many ideas, he brings together the theology of Moltmann and others that we discussed in chapter 1 and the philosophy of Wilber, integrating ideas that have their source in Hegel:

> In this way of seeing, God stands ahead of us in time, at the end of the journey, sending to us in waves, as it were, the gift of the present, an inrush of the future that pushes the past behind us and washes over us with a ceaseless flow of new possibilities, new options, new chances to rethink and receive new direction, new empowerment. This newness, these possibilities are always "at hand," "among us," and "coming" so we can "enter" the larger reality and transcend the space we currently fill–language you will recognize as being, again, the language of the kingdom of God, which is the language of the gospel.[295]

Like a recurring mantra, Emergent/postmodern teachers say "everything is evolving to a better future which will be the kingdom of God." But since they have dissociated their religion from all foundations, whether scientific or Biblical, their "theology of hope" is based on a humanly constructed "reality" that may not exist in this universe or any other one.

THE GOSPEL OF JESUS CHRIST

McLaren said that his idea of God dwelling in the future and pulling us ahead with new possibilities is the "language of the gospel." But it is not the gospel of Jesus Christ. It is a gospel of blind faith in ideas that

295 McLaren, *Generous*, 283.

offer no proof of their veracity. The real gospel is about sober truth, as Paul told Festus.

The gospel is, first of all, the gospel of Jesus Christ. We must define who Jesus is because there are many false doctrines of Christ in the world. Jesus existed as God and with God from all eternity (John 1:1). Jesus created the universe out of nothing (John 1:3; Hebrews 1:2). Jesus came into this world born of a virgin (Matthew 1:18-23). Jesus was fully human and fully God, the Son of God, and the Son of Man. He was the promised Jewish Messiah (Christ means "anointed one"). Jesus is unique, which is what "only begotten" means. He came in the flesh and was *not* an avatar with the "Christ spirit."

Jesus performed many miracles, the point of which was to prove His true identity as God incarnate. His contemporaries even admitted that no one had ever done works like He did. Jesus predicted his own resurrection from the dead. No other religious leader in history ever predicted and accomplished his own resurrection. Jesus bodily ascended into heaven and sits in the ultimate place of authority–at the right hand of God.

Jesus died on the cross because it was God's plan to execute His wrath against sin, not on the sinners who deserved it, but rather on His own Son: "*But the Lord was pleased To crush Him, putting Him to grief; If He would render Himself as a guilt offering, He will see His offspring, He will prolong His days, And the good pleasure of the Lord will prosper in His hand*" (**Isaiah 53:10**). Christians did not make up the idea of the substitutionary atonement because it pleased them; *God* declared it and executed it because it pleased *Him*.

The Bible says that the reason God poured out His wrath on His sinless Son was that He might be both the just and the justifier: "*whom God displayed publicly as a propitiation in His blood through faith. This was to demonstrate His righteousness, because in the forbearance of God He passed over the sins previously committed; for the demonstration, I say, of His righteousness at the present time, so that He would be just and the justifier of the one who has faith in Jesus*" (**Romans 3:25, 26**). The gospel is "good news" in the greatest possible way because it announces the terms whereby we may escape God's wrath against our sin and enjoy eternal fellowship with God and other believers.

This especially is true when we consider what we are escaping: "*and to give relief to you who are afflicted and to us as well when the Lord Jesus will be revealed from heaven with His mighty angels in flaming fire, dealing out retribution to those who do not know God and to those who do not obey the gospel of our Lord Jesus. These will pay the penalty of eternal destruction, away from the presence of the Lord and from the glory of His power*" (**2Thessalonians 1:7-9**). Future judgment is just as much the promise of God for the unrepentant as heaven is for believers.

To repent is to turn from serving sin, self, good works, religion, or anything to which we may be giving ultimacy, including vain ideas like those I have explained in this book. To repent is to turn from "vain idols" and "serve the living God" (1Thessalonians 1:9; Acts 14:15). To believe is not only to believe the truth about who Jesus is, but also to fully trust Him for salvation, the forgiveness of sins.

We have a choice. We can hope that Ken Wilber and his Emergent followers are right and that a better universe is emerging, or we can believe the testimony of Scripture and its real evidence in the real world. We can believe the Hegelian synthesis, or we can believe that opposites (one where God is coming in judgment and another where He is not) do not synthesize. One is true and the other is false. I believe the gospel as revealed in the Bible and reject the Emergent scheme that everything is getting better just because that is a preferred version of reality. I invite my readers to reject this postmodern fantasy world and turn to God through the gospel of Jesus Christ.

Conclusion

An Eschatology of Wishful Thinking

I agree with Tony Jones that the one factor unifying the Emergent movement is its eschatology. Yes, the movement is diverse. But it is the Emergent eschatology that makes the diversity possible. How? By making distinctive beliefs and practices unnecessary, since, in their thinking, the worst outcome we could imagine would only cause a temporary setback in the inevitable process of emergence. The "sin" that might cause such a setback is resistance to emergence - which Emergent followers by definition are not committing. Consequently, they are free to practice their religion any way they see fit. This means there is no limit to possible beliefs and practices.

Why do Emergent thinkers embrace this distinctive eschatology? Because of their romantic, idealistic inclinations. They wish to live in a world where everything is getting better—where God is drawing things toward a future that will be good for all of creation and devoid of cataclysmic judgment. The threat of such judgment, as they say with a sarcastic poke at Tim LaHaye, has been "left behind." Theirs is an eschatology of wishful thinking driven by human sentiment, not Biblical evidence. They see the world, as my Mom used to say, "through rose colored glasses." This entire movement does the same.

To reject the reality of future judgment is not merely to reject the beliefs of certain evangelicals who believe in literal Bible prophecy–it is to reject the beliefs expressed in nearly every Christian statement of faith throughout church history–beginning with the Apostle's Creed. Why would any Christian group reject such a Biblical, long-held belief? One answer seems most plausible: They dislike it. Jones says that they have an aversion to the idea of "darkness and gnashing of teeth." So do I. That is why I am trusting Jesus for salvation from God's future wrath.

Emergent thinking, as we have seen, is not new. It originated with Hegel. In Hegel's time, Romanticism arose as a rejection of the Enlightenment. Steven Kreis writes, "The Romantics returned God to Nature–the age revived the unseen world, the supernatural, the mysterious, the world of medieval man."[296] Kreis notices that Hegel and the Romantic period co-existed: "They saw history as a process of unfolding, a becoming. Was not this the upshot of what G. W. F. Hegel (1770-1831) had argued in his philosophy of history? And look at the time frame: Kant - 1780s, Hegel - 1820s and 30s." Now that another group (The Emergent Church) wishes to fight perceived influences of the Enlightenment they turn to a new Romanticism under the guidance of theological and philosophical followers and interpreters of Hegel (Moltmann and Wilber). They likewise do not like anything that de-mystifies the world, be it science or the Bible. Their mentally constructed world is infused with a mysterious God about whom we know little because He has not described Himself to us in words that anyone can understand. Emergent Romanticism thrives on the mysterious and unknown, imagining that something wonderful and ideal is unfolding and becoming, like the Romantics of old.

Romanticism is fine if restricted to art and fiction. But it is dangerous when applied to theology. Our eternal souls are too important to risk to an optimistic future that may not exist–and which the Bible says does not exist except for those who repent and believe the gospel. The Biblical authors give us certainty based not on human imagination, but on God's work through Christ who died for sins and was bodily raised from the dead. The human imagination is

296 http://www.historyguide.org/intellect/lecture16a.html (accessed August 1, 2008)

capable of building imaginary "worlds"; but humans cannot thereby make such mentally constructed worlds real.

The Bible speaks about those who base their beliefs on imagination: "*Thus says the Lord of hosts, 'Do not listen to the words of the prophets who are prophesying to you. They are leading you into futility; They speak a vision of their own imagination, Not from the mouth of the Lord'*" (**Jeremiah 23:16**). The issue in Jeremiah's day is the same issue that has arisen in our day because of the Emergent movement. Jeremiah prophesied coming judgment. Those who gained their insight from their own imaginations said it was not coming. The biblical apostles and prophets also have prophesied coming judgment and have issued warnings. They still speak authoritatively: "*While they are saying, "Peace and safety!" then destruction will come upon them suddenly like birth pangs upon a woman with child; and they shall not escape*" (**1Thessalonians 5:3**). The Emergent teachers are saying "peace and safety." Either the Biblical writers have spoken the truth or the Emergent writers have; but not both. In reality there is no synthesis of antithetical ideas. Our eternal souls depend upon whom we believe. I strongly urge my readers to believe the Biblical apostles and prophets. They alone have a proven track record of speaking the truth. Jeremiah has proven to be true, and Paul will be as well.

About the Author

Bob DeWaay is the senior pastor of Twin City Fellowship in Minneapolis, Minnesota. He has been a pastor with Twin City Fellowship for 28 years and the senior pastor since 1995. He holds a B.A. in Bible and Pastor Studies from North Central Bible College, and a M.A. in Theological Studies from Bethel Theological Seminary. Bob and his wife Diane have been married 36 years and have two children and two grandsons. He is the author of the book *Redefining Christianity – Understanding the Purpose Driven Movement.* Since 1992 Bob has published over 100 articles on important theological issues through Critical Issues Commentary. He is also a frequent radio guest on KKMS 980am in the Twin Cities and has a Critical Issues Commentary radio show on Oneplace.com. Bob also writes for the Christian Worldview Network.

Twin City Fellowship
P.O. Box 26127
Saint Louis Park, MN 55426
952-935-3100

www.cicministry.org
www.twincityfellowship.com